In
DESERT
PLACES

what happens when unlikely people in

unlikely places encounter the

presence of God

PAUL W.
CHAPPELL

First published in 2011 by Striving Together Publications, a
ministry of Lancaster Baptist Church, Lancaster, CA 93535.
Striving Together Publications is committed to providing
tried, trusted, and proven books that will further equip local
churches to carry out the Great Commission. Your comments
and suggestions are valued.

Striving Together Publications
4020 E. Lancaster Blvd.
Lancaster, CA 93535
800.201.7748

Cover design by Andrew Jones
Layout by Craig Parker
Edited by Monica Bass
Special thanks to our proofreaders.

ISBN 978-1-59894-161-6

Printed in the United States of America

CONTENTS

ACKNOWLEDGMENTS

I would like to first thank the wonderful Christians whose stories are shared in this book! Their lives are a continual encouragement to me and I count it a great privilege to serve the Lord with them.

Second, I want to thank Monica Bass for her countless hours and skilled efforts in helping to bring this manuscript to completion. Her godly spirit and gifted abilities have been invaluable to the process of making this book a reality.

Finally, I want to thank my family for expressing great faith during our twenty-five years in Lancaster. Thank you for taking this journey with me, and for following God with me through our own desert places!

FOREWORD

I well remember my first viewing of the land newly purchased by Lancaster Baptist Church. It was my first time in Lancaster and my first time to meet the young pastor of this church, Paul Chappell. Still in his early twenties, Pastor Chappell had recently led the church to purchase twenty acres of land to expand their growing ministry, and he was so excited to show it to me. As we drove out of town toward the property, I noticed a large desert lot of *nothing*.

With great enthusiasm, Pastor Chappell pointed toward that very lot. "That's it, Dr. Sisk!"

"That's really something," I responded. But inwardly I wondered, *How can he get so excited about a dust bowl with Joshua trees and tumbleweeds?*

That was over twenty years ago.

When I approach this same lot today, I see in substance what Pastor Chappell saw by faith twenty years ago—a beautiful, well-maintained eighty acre campus with a thriving church and Bible college. In this desert place, thousands of people have found the answer for their lives and the hope of their eternity. In this desert place, hundreds have been trained to minister as servant leaders, carrying the Gospel and planting churches around the world.

It has been my joyful privilege over the past twenty years to watch as the dust bowl has been transformed into a beautiful desert oasis. Particularly, it has been my joy to know Pastor Chappell. Since the early days when I first preached for him until now, I have closely observed as Dr. Chappell has grown from a young pastor with a heart for God and a love for people to an influential international leader. Over the past ten years, I have been blessed to call Dr. Chappell my pastor.

As the ministry here has grown, I've noticed that Pastor's demeanor has not changed. His example of and emphasis on servant leadership has permeated the ministry for the entire twenty-five years he has served here. Even as you read in this book the stories of wonderful conversions and miraculous provisions, you will see the heart of a man who is very careful to give the glory to God.

In Desert Places does not exalt man but resonates with the wonderful things God can do through those totally dedicated to Him. Reading this manuscript invoked tears, laughter, joy, and thanksgiving.

This book will be a source of great encouragement to all who read it. It will strengthen your faith. It will increase your desire to reach more people with the Gospel of the Lord Jesus Christ. It will cause you to rejoice in the power or our great God.

After you have read this book, you will by all means desire to read it again. You will think of others who would be encouraged and helped by it. The thrilling stories of how God used many Bible characters in desert places intertwined with the testimonies of people in Lancaster Baptist Church are faith-building and God-honoring. They will provide hope for all who labor in desert places.

Don Sisk
President/Director emeritus of BIMI
Chairman of the Missions Department of West Coast Baptist College

INTRODUCTION

What would you expect in the desert? Parched, cracked soil? Barren wastelands? Coyotes and rattlesnakes? Yes, that's about right. No one anticipates much growth or change here. It's dry, desolate, and barren.

Unless...

...the desert is transformed by the presence of God.

Yes, God's presence can transform even desert places.

Scripture records numerous accounts of God's intervention in desert places. These accounts indicate that God actually chooses the most unlikely people and unlikely places to display His glory.

And God's presence is still transforming desert places today. That is what this book is all about. It's the true story of God's incredible work in a desert place.

Lancaster Baptist Church is situated in a literal desert—the Mojave Desert of Southern California. Twenty-five years ago, when this story begins, there wasn't much to our church—a dilapidated building in foreclosure, a mountain of debt, a small community, and a handful of people who wanted to see God work.

Today, we minister on an eighty-acre desert campus, beautifully landscaped with numerous large buildings. The buildings house the most important desert transformations— changed lives.

And it is these lives that are the real story of this book. You see, *desert places* can be literal or representative. Indeed, God can transform a literal desert. But He can also transform desert lives.

Let me explain.

Every picture begins with a blank canvas. No one walks up to the canvas and admires its beauty. There's nothing there *to* admire. In fact, no one but an artist even sees potential in the empty canvas.

Likewise, every miraculous story begins with a desert place— an empty, barren, and maybe even desolate place. It appears unlikely and unable to support growth or change.

The desert landscapes of our lives represent any time when our canvas is blank. These are times when our plans come to an end, our agendas are put on hold, or we don't know what's next. We feel barren and dry. These places could represent trials, seasons of transition, unexpected circumstances, or any place where we have questions and uncertainty.

It's at these times and in these places that God takes our blank canvases and paints them with His incomparable artistry. He transforms our deserts into lush gardens of beauty.

So, yes, in a literal sense, God has transformed our desert. But in a much greater sense, He's stepped into individual lives and filled them with unexplainable beauty.

In this book, you will read the stories of people—unlikely people—who found themselves in desert places. Apart from God, the outcome of their lives would have been empty. But, as you will see, God's presence makes all the difference.

These stories tell of the numerous works God does in desert places. He multiplies. He mends. He binds wounds. He restores relationships. He offers solitude and refreshment. In short, He does the unlikely—the impossible—in desert places.

And the very starting places for these miracles prove that it is God's presence alone that makes the difference. Not God plus a really great idea, or God plus a likely occurrence, or God plus talent. It's just God.

Perhaps you are in a desert place. This book holds good news for you: God delights in working desert miracles!

Many of the greatest men in Scripture found themselves in desert places—Moses, Philip, John the Baptist, David, Jeremiah, even Christ Himself. In this book, we enter a desert classroom and through the pages of Scripture discover what the desert teaches us about the presence of our God and the work He does in and through us in desert places.

I pray that through these real life testimonies of what happens when unlikely people in unlikely places encounter the presence of God, you will be encouraged to seek the presence of God in *your* desert.

Even in desert places—*especially* in desert places—God still moves.

ONE

DESERT SUNRISE
WHEN MINISTRY BEGINS

I never guessed on that Sunday night when I unknowingly candidated for a small church in an out-of-the-way desert town what God was about to do through this struggling church with just a handful of people. What I thought was a simple favor to a friend—preaching in his church when our family passed through the area on vacation—became the dawn of a whole new day of ministry for my family.

After I preached that Sunday night service, my friend asked our family to step outside while he had a moment with the congregation. After dismissing the service, he joined us on the front steps a few minutes later and invited us to Burger King. There we encountered the shock of our lives when he informed us that he was resigning and the church had just unanimously voted me in as the new pastor.

It didn't take long to overcome the shock, however. I simply declined and informed my friend that I had no desire to pastor in this desert town. I was already on staff at a vibrant, growing church in northern California, and I was secure in that ministry.

The following morning, Terrie and I settled our two children into the backseat of the car and resumed our vacation. As we drove out of town, I noticed new construction and housing developments. For Sale signs, liberally sprinkled throughout the community, marked houses ready for occupants. Gently, the Holy Spirit pricked my soul, "This city is preparing for growth, and it needs a Bible-preaching, Baptist church."

Neither Terrie nor I said much as we drove toward the Sequoia National Forest. Danielle and Larry enjoyed the scenery from the back seat—in surprisingly quiet fashion for a three-year-old and a two-year-old.

Several hours later, under the canopy of giant redwoods, I reached for Terrie's hand, not really sure how to put my heart into words…or what her reaction might be. "Honey, I don't know how to explain this, but I really believe that God is touching my heart for the Lancaster area. I believe He wants us to accept the call to that church."

With a look that almost expressed relief, Terrie returned the squeeze. "I've been feeling the same way for the past few hours. I wondered how to tell you."

We had no idea what this new ministry would hold. We knew the obvious: The church was small—twelve members voted us in. The church was struggling financially—they were meeting in the upstairs portion of a dilapidated building downtown and had no money available for a pastor's salary.

There were more difficulties nobody mentioned, but we would learn those soon enough.

In that moment, however, when Terrie and I yielded our hearts to God's call, none of those things mattered. We knew we belonged to a God who delights in working miracles in desert places. And we were eager to see what He would do.

The sun was just beginning to rise over a new ministry in a desert place.

DESERT WELCOME

"Chappell, you're making a big mistake, brother!" I heard over the CB radio from the Ryder truck behind us. Dave, a friend from our church in northern California had helped us load our belongings into the moving truck, and now he was willingly giving his energy to help us get started in this new ministry. He followed Terrie, the children, and me as we drove our blue Mitsubishi station wagon to Lancaster. Seated in the truck next to Dave was Cary, a senior at the high school from our home church. I'm not sure what Dave was expecting, but as we entered the western portion of our desert valley on Avenue D, he was apparently disappointed.

The CB radio crackled again, "There's nothing here. I see the sign for Lancaster, but I don't see a town. This is a wasteland with nothing but tumbleweeds. I can hardly keep the truck on the road for the wind. Turn back—it's not too late to go back north."

I looked across the wind-swept desert. Dave was right. There *wasn't* much to look at. If ministry in this area was going to be as fruitless as the withered grass and blowing tumbleweeds across the brown expanse before us, it would be a waste.

DESERT PLACE CALLINGS

I've learned that God sees deserts differently than we do. He sees the sandy wastelands of our lives as the launching pad for ministry miracles. In many lives, desert places have been the very spots first touched by the sunrise of fruitful ministry.

Consider, for example, a place Scripture calls "the backside of the desert" (Exodus 3:1). This desert is much like others— dry, hot, dusty, monotonous. For forty years, Moses searched out desert herbage for his flocks as he tended sheep in this remote location.

Many years earlier, Moses had been miraculously spared from the Nile crocodiles as a baby. Thanks to the faith of his parents and the providential hand of God, Pharaoh's daughter found three-month-old baby Moses in a bulrush basket by the brink of the Nile. She adopted him and raised him in the palace (Exodus 2:1–10).

At age forty, however, Moses made a life-changing decision: "By faith Moses, when he was come to years, refused to be called the son of Pharaoh's daughter; Choosing rather to suffer affliction with the people of God, than to enjoy the pleasures of sin for a season; Esteeming the reproach of Christ greater riches than the treasures in Egypt: for he had respect unto the recompence of the reward" (Hebrews 11:24–26).

One might think Moses' decision to choose the reproach of Christ over the affluence of Pharaoh's court would spark the dawn of his miraculous ministry. Indeed, it might have, but his sunrise quickly faded when, in his zeal to follow through on his commitment, he murdered an Egyptian. Forced to flee to the desert for safety, he tended sheep in the wilderness for the next forty years.

AN EXTRAORDINARY PLACE

What disappointment must have shaped the landscape of Moses' future! What sandstorms of doubt must have burned through his mind! Gradually, he settled into desert routines. He married and accepted this barren location as his lot in life. For forty years, Moses faithfully fed his flocks on the backside of the desert.

Then one ordinary day, in a matter of a few miraculous moments, Moses' desert was transformed by a burning bush—the flaming presence of God. Exodus 3:1–12 records the story:

> *Now Moses kept the flock of Jethro his father in law, the priest of Midian: and he led the flock to the backside of the desert, and came to the mountain of God, even to Horeb. And the angel of the LORD appeared unto him in a flame of fire out of the midst of a bush: and he looked, and, behold, the bush burned with fire, and the bush was not consumed. And Moses said, I will now turn aside, and see this great sight, why the bush is not burnt. And when the LORD saw that he turned aside to see, God called unto him out of the midst of the bush, and said, Moses, Moses. And he said, Here am I. And he said, Draw not nigh hither: put off thy shoes from*

off thy feet, for the place whereon thou standest is holy ground. Moreover he said, I am the God of thy father, the God of Abraham, the God of Isaac, and the God of Jacob. And Moses hid his face; for he was afraid to look upon God.

And the LORD said, I have surely seen the affliction of my people which are in Egypt, and have heard their cry by reason of their taskmasters; for I know their sorrows; And I am come down to deliver them out of the hand of the Egyptians, and to bring them up out of that land unto a good land and a large, unto a land flowing with milk and honey; unto the place of the Canaanites, and the Hittites, and the Amorites, and the Perizzites, and the Hivites, and the Jebusites. Now therefore, behold, the cry of the children of Israel is come unto me: and I have also seen the oppression wherewith the Egyptians oppress them. Come now therefore, and I will send thee unto Pharaoh, that thou mayest bring forth my people the children of Israel out of Egypt.

And Moses said unto God, Who am I, that I should go unto Pharaoh, and that I should bring forth the children of Israel out of Egypt? And he said, Certainly I will be with thee; and this shall be a token unto thee, that I have sent thee: When thou hast brought forth the people out of Egypt, ye shall serve God upon this mountain.

Moses' desert experience at the burning bush presents an important desert lesson, one of the first Terrie and I learned in

Lancaster: Never take for granted a place where God is working in your heart.

Yes, the desert is a barren place, but when God works there, it is transformed into an extraordinary place.

When Terrie and I first arrived at our Lancaster apartment with the Ryder truck, it was hard to see this place where God had led us as extraordinary. There was no welcome party—only one man from our new church to help us move in. It was early July, and it must have been well over one hundred degrees outside.

Terrie's eyes filled with tears as she stepped into our stuffy, non-air conditioned, well-soiled apartment. The aged appliances, rough neighborhood, and animal stained (and scented) carpet did little to excite her about living in the desert.

Never take for granted a place where God is working in your heart.

With the fortitude of a desert warrior, Terrie directed Dave, Cary, and me to wedge our mattress into the small bedroom and store the too-large frame and headboard in the dilapidated one-car garage. In fact, about half of our furniture found a home in the garage that afternoon. The tiny living room and two bedrooms just couldn't hold even the small amount of furniture we had brought with us.

Little did we know with what joy and gratefulness we would eventually celebrate that day we moved to the desert. We couldn't begin to imagine then how special the Mojave Desert would later become to us. If we could have known, we would have rejoiced in its barrenness, anticipating the miracles of growth God was about to perform.

A PLACE OF DESOLATION

When you live in the desert, it's hard to romanticize its beauty. Moses later referred to the desert of Sinai, where he met the Lord, as "that great and terrible wilderness" (Deuteronomy 1:19; 8:15) and "the waste howling wilderness" (Deuteronomy 32:10). Jeremiah 2:6 further elaborates, describing this wilderness as "a land of deserts and of pits...a land of drought, and of the shadow of death...a land that no man passed through, and where no man dwelt."

The desert's desolation is an incredible backdrop for the wonders of God.

Nobody was clamoring for the opportunity to pastor in Lancaster, California, when God called our family there in 1986. Not only did the pastor before me seem desperate to move out, but my friends told us we were making a mistake—and the most obvious circumstances might have indicated they were right.

God, however, thought differently. Here He has raised up a church that is substantially touching our community for the glory of God, and through this church He has changed countless lives by the power of His Spirit.

We tend to perceive "desert place" callings as a mistake, but the desert's desolation is an incredible backdrop for the wonders of God. For the "backside of the desert" is also home to "the mountain of God" (Exodus 3:1).

Lonely, desolate deserts are opportunities to meet God—places to connect our insufficiency with His incredible power. But this divine connection requires a choice.

A PLACE OF DECISION

When Moses stood before the burning bush, he was eighty years old. God's call to lead Israel to the Promised Land must have seemed impossible—and tiring. He could have chosen to retire right where he was. Surely feeding sheep was easier than leading more than two million people through the wilderness. In fact, Moses nearly rejected God's call because of his fear.

Forty years earlier, Moses had already made a difficult choice, casting in his lot with the Lord and identifying himself with God's people. That choice proved to be a turning point in Moses' life. But now, he would have to choose again. This is ultimately the inception of every ministry—a choice, a decision to trust and follow God.

Moses' life is testimony to the fact that being surrendered to the Lord is a life-long process. A single choice isn't enough; living for God must become a *daily* choice. Yet, his desert calling and decision for God also reminds us that choosing to answer God's call is the dawning of a new day.

Desert decisions are unique in that they pave the way to lead others to a similar decision. In the very desert where Moses made his choice, he would soon lead two million Israelites to that very spot—Mount Horeb, also called Mount Sinai. Here the entire nation of Israel would also face the decision of dedication to their God.

So, when God called Moses to make a desert decision, He had more in mind than Moses could dream. Moses' decision was the gate through which God would later lead His people to also decide for Him.

Today, God calls each of us to the decision of dedication. He implores us to choose to give ourselves wholly to Him. Romans 12:1–2 says, "I beseech you therefore, brethren, by the mercies of God, that ye present your bodies a living sacrifice, holy, acceptable unto God, which is your reasonable service. And be not conformed to this world: but be ye transformed by the renewing of your mind, that ye may prove what is that good, and acceptable, and perfect, will of God."

We never know the future of our decisions, but the decision to surrender is the starting place for desert transformation.

The desert has been a place of decision for many. I'm thankful Terrie and I yielded to the Lord and answered His call to desert ministry. Perhaps you're in the desert, standing at a place of decision. Choose the path of total dedication. It's a decision we've never regretted.

DESERT HOPE

Why did God call Moses? What would move God to seek out a backwards, stuttering outcast and supernaturally empower him to lead over two million stubborn, complaining people out of Egypt?

Exodus 3:7 provides an answer: "I have surely seen the affliction of my people which *are* in Egypt, and have heard their cry by reason of their taskmasters; for I know their sorrows." God saw the affliction of His people, and He moved to meet their needs.

God's desert calling for Moses was God's answer to the afflicted cry of His people. And when Moses answered God's call with a decision of surrender, an opportunity of deliverance opened for the Israelites.

Jesus demonstrated the same heart of love in His earthly ministry. Mark 6:34 records, "And Jesus, when he came out, saw much people, and was moved with compassion toward them, because they were as sheep not having a shepherd: and he began to teach them many things."

The decision to surrender is the starting place for desert transformation.

I wonder what God saw in Lancaster when He called our family to pastor in the Antelope Valley. Perhaps it was a teenage gang member whose crime-infested heart was growing desperate for hope. Perhaps it was a weeping young couple whose infant daughter was given little chance for survival. Perhaps it was the owner of a liquor store whose hardened heart and empty days needed to be filled with Christ. Perhaps it was a divorced man and woman whose wounded, broken hearts could only be restored to each other by the amazing, healing grace of God.

All of these people, and many more besides, have been reached by the ministry of Lancaster Baptist Church. Their stories are told in these pages as a testimony to the grace of God to touch lives and the power of God to work in desert places.

When one individual says "yes" to God's call, a day of hope dawns for others. It's a desert sunrise—where ministry begins.

T W O

DESERT COMMISSION
WHAT MINISTRY MEANS

The call to Lancaster may have been a desert sunrise, but in those early days, the first streaks of dawn sometimes appeared pretty faint.

My first administrative duty as a new pastor was to mow the parking lot—yes, I said it right, *mow*. The weeds really were that thick across the cracked concrete. The building also was in serious need of renovation, so Terrie and I emptied our meager savings account and invested it into making the property a more attractive setting for visitors to hear the Gospel.

Cary, the high school student who rode with Dave in the Ryder truck, asked if he could stay for a couple of weeks to help us get started. Together, we built a makeshift platform and set up a sound system in the auditorium. We ripped out the carpet in the halls that had been patched with long strips of duct tape, and we painted the concrete floor. We also replaced the shredded curtains, removed the already peeling wallpaper, and painted the walls. Next, we cleared a tiny room for a church office, and I filled the shelves with my small library.

The next morning, my whistling entry into my new office was abruptly silenced by the handiwork of a vandal. I can't describe the discouragement I felt when I saw the desk covered with a crumpled heap of Kool-Aid drenched papers. The floor was littered with torn books, thrown from the shelves. Our newly purchased sound system was stolen as well. It seemed that every effort for progress was immediately countered with a setback.

The vandalism was demoralizing, but the financial difficulties we soon faced carried even greater weight for our small church. I had understood when I accepted the call to this church that the finances were slim, but I didn't realize they were actually perilous. I learned of these troubles the hard way.

If anything of eternal significance were to happen in this place, it would be by the power of God's Spirit.

Within days of our arrival, I wrote a Gospel tract and took it to a local printer. "There's no way I'm doing more work for that church," the printer spat. "You already owe me two thousand dollars!" With an already depleted savings account and no salary, this was difficult news. But I promised the man that if he would print five thousand tracts, we would pay for them and eventually pay off the rest of the church's account. Somehow he believed me.

Nobody had warned me of any outstanding bills, but I soon learned there was a full ledger column of them, only they weren't entered in a ledger. I had to discover and work through each outstanding account one by one. The clincher came when I encountered a man walking through the church hallway with a spiral notebook and a pencil. "Can I help you?" I asked. "I'm from the bank," he explained. "I'm just appraising the building for foreclosure." Foreclosure?! My heart sank to the floor.

Through all the confusing setbacks of our start in Lancaster, there was one truth that etched itself deeply in our hearts: if anything of eternal significance were to happen in this place, it would be by the power of God's Spirit.

God delights in choosing people and places the world would consider useless and insignificant, and transforming them into instruments for His service.

> *For ye see your calling, brethren, how that not many wise men after the flesh, not many mighty, not many noble, are called: But God hath chosen the foolish things of the world to confound the wise; and God hath chosen the weak things of the world to confound the things which are mighty; And base things of the world, and things which are despised, hath God chosen, yea, and things which are not, to bring to nought things that are:*—1 CORINTHIANS 1:26–28

This is what God did with Moses. Who could have dreamed that God would choose *him*—a backwards shepherd—to deliver God's people from bondage?

UNLIKELY SELECTIONS

Why does God commission unlikely people to do His work? Actually, that's all He has to choose from! None of us has the wisdom or the strength to accomplish God's work alone. We sometimes think we can do it. But when we try in our own strength, we, like Moses, soon find ourselves stranded in the desert. It is only when we *realize* our insufficiency—when we come face to face with our weakness—that we become candidates for God's power.

God chooses weak people so that His work will be carried out "Not by might, nor by power, but by my spirit, saith the LORD of hosts" (Zechariah 4:6).

Without divine enabling, Moses didn't have what it would take. How was an eighty-year-old social outcast who stuttered supposed to lead over two million people in mass exodus from Egypt, across the desert, and into the land of Canaan? Only by the power of God.

CALLED TO FOLLOW

Surprisingly, God didn't begin Moses' commission with direction to lead the people out of Egypt. He prefaced it with a call to Himself: "Come now therefore, and I will send thee unto Pharaoh…" (Exodus 3:10). God was going to send Moses to Pharaoh, but first, He called Moses to draw near to Himself.

Consider the implication of God's order: Far from being like the taskmasters in Egypt who cared only of physical production, God desired a relationship with Moses.

This is incredible. God has every right to demand our service. He created us. He redeemed us. But He is interested in so much more than what we do for Him. Included in God's commission for our lives is the call to know Him and develop an intimate relationship with Him.

Many people are busy *doing* the work of God, but never take time *being* the personal followers of God. God never intended to thrust us into the rigors of ministry without providing the sustaining help of intimacy with Him. Furthermore, we cannot effectively do God's work when we don't really know Him.

Before God sends us to communicate His message to others—across the street or around the world—He first commissions us to know and

> *God never intended to thrust us into the rigors of ministry without providing the sustaining help of intimacy with Him.*

follow Him. Even Jesus followed this pattern. He beckoned His disciples with the words, "Follow me, and I will make you fishers of men" (Matthew 4:19). The task of transforming these rough fishermen into compassionate soulwinners required that they first learn Christ's heart and methods. Thus equipped, they shook the world for Christ.

I've had the privilege of attending the graduation ceremony for men in our church who have graduated from the Los Angeles County Sheriff's Academy. During the ceremony, it always fascinates me to hear the recitation of the department's philosophies and principles that the deputies have been required to memorize. It's as if the sheriff's department says, "Before we strap a gun to your hip and assign you a car, you must learn the philosophies of this department." They cannot afford to have thousands of deputies throughout the county shooting first and asking questions later. Before the department will pin the badge on, they insist that the deputies satisfactorily learn the philosophies and policies of the department.

In a similar way, before we attempt to serve others in the Lord's name, we must first learn to follow Him. We must know Him, and our ministry must reflect His heart of compassion. Jesus said in John 12:26, "If any man serve me, let him follow me...." *Following* Christ is a prerequisite for *serving* Christ.

COMMISSIONED TO GO

In the same breath that God commissioned Moses to follow Him, He further instructed, "...and I will send thee unto Pharaoh..." (Exodus 3:10). God calls us to follow Him because He has a purpose—a commission—for our lives.

I remember in vivid detail the day I was saved—April 5, 1972. That moment when, as a ten-year-old boy, I trusted Christ is the cornerstone of my relationship with the Lord. Another event of sacred importance to me is the day I was called to preach. As a seventh-grade boy at church camp in Palmer Lake, Colorado, I understood that God had created me with a purpose and wanted me to commit my life to His service. I also understood that He wanted me to dedicate my life to preaching the Gospel.

In the past thirty years of ministry, I've had countless opportunities to lead others to Christ. What a joy it has been for me to teach these new Christians that God has a special purpose for their lives as well. The individual details of God's calling vary from person to person. Some will serve in a full-time ministry capacity such as a pastor or a missionary, and some will be a witness for Christ at their workplace or in their business. But everyone's purpose is wrapped around Christ's commission to tell others of His saving grace.

Christ gave the local church the responsibility to bring the Gospel to all the world. We call it the Great Commission:

> *And Jesus came and spake unto them, saying, All power is given unto me in heaven and in earth. Go ye therefore, and teach all nations, baptizing them in the name of the Father, and of the Son, and of the Holy Ghost: Teaching them to observe all things whatsoever I have commanded you: and, lo, I am with you alway, even unto the end of the world. Amen.*—MATTHEW 28:18–20

Second Peter 3:9 reveals the motivation of Christ's commission: "The Lord is…not willing that any should perish, but that all should come to repentance." God's purpose is to draw all men and women to Himself, and His plan is to use us to do it.

Just as God commissioned Moses to lead the Israelites from the physical bondage of slavery, so He has commissioned us to lead others from the spiritual bondage of sin.

Terrie and I moved to Lancaster, California, to obey this commission. During the first year of our ministry in Lancaster, I personally knocked on five hundred doors per week, bringing the Gospel from house to house. I encouraged men in our church to join me, and I trained them how to lead a person to Christ. God has blessed our church's focus on soulwinning. Today there are men and women all throughout the Antelope Valley who first heard the Gospel through the ministry of Lancaster Baptist Church, trusted Christ as Saviour, and are now committed to obeying the Great Commission. They faithfully witness for Christ to family members, friends, neighbors, and co-workers. Several times a week, church members meet for organized soulwinning during which they bring the Gospel from house to house in our community.

When a person understands his purpose in life—to obey Christ's commission—it enables him to know the fulfillment of living the life God designed for him. When we, like Moses, obey His commission, we experience the joy of God touching other lives through us.

WHY GOD DELIVERS DESERT COMMISSIONS

God's commission to Moses was a response to the plight of the Israelites' slavery in Egypt. In Exodus 3:10, God revealed His heart of compassion as He explained His purpose to Moses: "…that thou mayest bring forth my people the children of Israel out of Egypt."

Understand the significance of this truth: God commissions us because He wants to give to others. When a person obeys God's commission, others' lives are changed—forever. And, in

God's plan, those impacted are soon commissioned and given the opportunity to impact others.

Through Moses, God was about to lead His people on an incredible, adventurous journey. But wasn't this a bit much for the trembling shepherd who stood before the burning bush? Was Moses really up to the task?

HOW GOD EQUIPS US

God's commission for Moses stretched him beyond what he thought possible. In fact, it *was* beyond Moses' ability—were he required to accomplish it on his own. God's commission for us is always far greater than our ability, but it is never greater than what He can do through us.

Quite frankly, the ministry is overwhelming. When I arrived in Lancaster as a twenty-four-year-old pastor, I immediately recognized that the problems sprawled before me were far beyond my power to solve. Back then, I assumed that as I grew older, the problems would become easier. But as the Lord has blessed our church with growth, the needs have actually enlarged. The ministry is still overwhelming!

I have learned, however, that the presence of God makes all the difference. Over and over again, I've watched God fulfill the promise He made to Moses. When Moses pointed out his inability to fill God's commission, the Lord answered, "Certainly I will be with thee" (Exodus 3:12).

CERTAINLY

I like that word *certainly*. If God had only used the words, "I will be with thee," that would be an incredible promise. But, knowing our tendency to fear and our need for reassurance, He prefaced His promise with the word *certainly*. However small our faith, however empty our resources, He will certainly be with us.

God will never call us and then leave us in a lonely position. Over the past twenty-five years, I have often claimed the promise of Hebrews 13:5–6, "I will never leave thee, nor forsake thee. So that we may boldly say, The Lord is my helper, and I will not fear what man shall do unto me." Because He has certainly promised to be with us, we can boldly stake our ministry on His words.

When you receive a desert commission and are tempted to sink in despair, make no mistake—God will be with you.

THE GREAT I AM

Desert ministry—miraculous ministry—is far bigger than we are. Moses saw this instantly, and he protested that he was insufficient to the commission. Even after God promised His certain presence, Moses had questions: How could he convince the Israelites that they should follow him? How should he describe the God who called him? Bringing the Israelites through the wilderness would be an incredible job. And Moses knew that just the first step—convincing them to leave Egypt— would be equally impossible.

God answered Moses' questions with a description of Himself: "And God said unto Moses, I AM THAT I AM: and he said, Thus shalt thou say unto the children of Israel, I AM hath sent me unto you" (Exodus 3:14). In this statement, God revealed a crucial ministry equation: God's presence equals God's provision.

I AM THAT I AM says it all. It declares God as the eternal, self-existent one who is in Himself everything we need. Human sources of provision will eventually run dry in the desert. But God Himself never fails, and He continuously supplies all resources necessary to obey His commission.

WHAT IS IN YOUR HAND?

Moses knew he had God's presence and His provision, but he still had a question: What if the Israelites would not believe him? Standing before a burning, but unconsumed bush, *Moses* knew for sure that God was speaking to him. But what about when he returned to Egypt? How would *the people* know?

This time, God answered Moses' question with a question: "What is that in thine hand?" (Exodus 4:2). What happened next was far beyond what Moses could have expected:

> *And the LORD said unto him, What is that in thine hand? And he said, A rod. And he said, Cast it on the ground. And he cast it on the ground, and it became a serpent; and Moses fled from before it. And the LORD said unto Moses, Put forth thine hand, and take it by the tail. And he put forth his hand, and caught it, and*

it became a rod in his hand: That they may believe that the LORD God of their fathers, the God of Abraham, the God of Isaac, and the God of Jacob, hath appeared unto thee.

And the LORD said furthermore unto him, Put now thine hand into thy bosom. And he put his hand into his bosom: and when he took it out, behold, his hand was leprous as snow. And he said, Put thine hand into thy bosom again. And he put his hand into his bosom again; and plucked it out of his bosom, and, behold, it was turned again as his other flesh.—EXODUS 4:2–7

God takes us just as we are when we give Him all we have, and He does wonders. The power of God to turn a rod into a serpent and back into a rod again and to cause a hand to become leprous and then heal it is astonishing. But even more astonishing than *what* God does, is through *whom* He does it. God channels His power through human instruments. We—you and I—get to be the conduits through which the power of God touches other lives!

OPPORTUNITY IN THE DESERT

Without God's power, a desert commission is impossible. But with God's power, there is no limit to what God will produce in the desert. In God's desert commissions, He simply asks us to give Him what is in our hand—to surrender all that He has already given to us—and then He miraculously produces spiritual fruit through us.

It's been twenty-five years now since a vandal baptized our first church office in Kool-Aid and the bank prepared for foreclosure. By God's grace, we are still fulfilling God's commission to tell others of His saving grace. By His Spirit, we have seen Him use our church to touch countless lives with His power. We've

Even more astonishing than what God does, is through whom He does it.

seen people delivered from sin, sacrificially dedicate their all, and develop in the grace of God. But it has all been by God's power and to God's glory.

A desert commission might be overwhelming, but it is an opportunity to see the miraculous work of God.

THREE

DESERT DISCOVERIES
WHERE AUTHENTIC MINISTRY LEADS

W hen I first looked across the Mojave Desert through the dusty windshield of our blue Mitsubishi station wagon, I thought I had seen it all in one glance— sand, tumbleweeds, and Joshua trees. Pretty mundane.

But I quickly learned that the desert is full of surprises. With changing weather, unexpected wildflowers, and even hidden reptiles, the desert isn't as routine as it first appears.

Moses knew the desert well. He spent forty years herding sheep across its wastelands, and he was so familiar with its irregularities that he could predict them. It was a surprise beyond even his experience, however, that arrested Moses' attention at the burning bush.

This bush led Moses to a discovery that would change his life completely. On this holy ground, he would learn the nature of his God—a discovery that is the foundation for all fruit-producing desert ministry.

A POWERFUL GOD

And Moses said, I will now turn aside, and see this great sight, why the bush is not burnt.—EXODUS 3:3

Moses knew that brush fires are common in the desert. So what drew him aside to see the burning bush? And what was its significance? The burning bush is an incredible symbol of power. The fire represented God's deity, and the bush not being consumed by the fire was an evidence of God's protection.

Forty years earlier, Moses had thought he could deliver his people by his own strength (Acts 7:23–29), but by the time he reached the burning bush, he had long since given up that hope. Now Moses was to learn that God *did* want him to deliver the Israelites—by God's power.

God's call to Moses on the backside of the desert was proof that the ministry is God's idea, not ours. Were the ministry our own idea, it would end with the same futile effects as Moses' earlier effort to protect his fellow Israelite by murdering the Egyptian (Exodus 2:11–15). But because it is God's idea, it can survive the harsh desert climates and bear fruit in the lonely wilderness.

DESERT MINISTRY

If I had written a script for my ministry when I first surrendered to preach as a seventh-grade boy, I would not have included a desert calling to a small, floundering church. But through that very call, I've seen firsthand that spiritual increase in ministry is limitless when it is produced by the Holy Spirit of God.

My desire has been that our church would reach as many people as possible with the Gospel. We have prayed that each of these new Christians would grow in grace and that they would discover God in a personal, vibrant relationship. Ministry carried out by God's principles reflects God's nature. Authentic, biblical ministry brings people to a discovery of God.

Many today try to build and operate the church with fleshly creativity. This ministry philosophy takes God's original idea—the ministry itself—and attempts to carry it out by man's effort, as though it were nothing more than an entrepreneurial enterprise. In such churches, community surveys, rock bands, and trendy technology gather a crowd and boost attendance. This kind of growth, however, cannot bear lasting spiritual fruit.

Soulwinning, discipleship, preaching—these are God's ideas. This is His blueprint for ministry. And this is what I came to Lancaster to do. My goal wasn't to build the largest church but to build lives for Christ through the power of the Gospel.

When we try to measure success by worldly standards, we're doomed to failure or destined to compromise. But when we follow God's plan, He promises to bless by the power of His Spirit. I'm thankful for the opportunity to see the wind of God's Spirit sweep across tumbleweed covered terrain and change people's lives.

HEAD-ON ENCOUNTER

I had never seen someone more angry than Linda Bishop was when she came to visit my office. "What kind of a cult are you running here anyway?" she stormed, as she slammed her fist down on my desk.

This was a first for me, and I didn't remember anyone in Bible college telling me how to handle it. "Let's pray," I suggested quickly. I don't think Linda bowed her head, and I'm not sure what I said, but I was counting on the Lord to read between the lines!

As soon as I finished, Linda picked up right where she had left off. As she continued venting her frustration, the situation became clear.

It all started with Linda's in-laws, Ray and Juanita Bishop. Both had been saved in their teen years but had not become grounded in a church or in their relationship with the Lord. But several months earlier, they had visited Lancaster Baptist Church. Here they found the conditions they needed to flourish spiritually. They joined and immediately blossomed. They soaked up the teaching and preaching and began going soulwinning to reach others.

The ministry is God's idea—not ours.

A few months later, primarily through Ray and Juanita's influence and prayers, Linda's unsaved son and his girlfriend visited our church. Jeff and Marilee were soon saved and baptized and began coming to church faithfully. They married and determined to establish a Christian home.

Jeff and Marilee *loved* church, and they enthusiastically got involved. They came to Sunday school, the morning service, the Sunday evening service, and Wednesday night Bible study.

Jeff even began going out soulwinning on Tuesday evenings, and together, they decided to begin tithing. Their lives were blossoming, and they were full of the joy of the Lord.

One evening, soon after Marilee gave birth to a beautiful little girl, Linda called and asked for Jeff.

"He's not home," Marilee responded. "He's out soulwinning with men from the church."

"Doing *what*?!" Linda wasn't happy. For one thing, the couple was renting an apartment in a shady part of town, and she didn't like to think of Marilee and the baby being left alone at night. Then, going *soulhunting* (as she misunderstood the word), whatever that might be, sounded pretty fanatical. She didn't say much more to Marilee about it, but she had a lot to say to me a few days later as she came to my office!

"So," Linda continued fuming in my office, "what's this with you teaching my son to go *soulhunting* and pulling him away from his home where he ought to be with his wife? And why are you telling my kids—who can't even afford a decent place to live—that they need to be giving all their money to the church? You...you..." she began to struggle for words. "You're ruining my family and running a cult!"

She paused, and I took the opportunity to interject. "Linda,

Authentic, biblical ministry brings people to a discovery of God.

there's only one way you can really know what's going on here. Why don't you come to a church service and see for yourself what I'm preaching and your kids are learning."

A SPIRIT-FILLED DIFFERENCE

That evening, Linda told her husband, Rick, that she had been in to see me, and she suggested they take me up on my challenge to visit the church. Rick was often on the road on weekends for work, so it was several weeks before they made it to church.

Rick and Linda visited on a Sunday evening, the night of our annual Easter musical. The choir and drama team presented a dramatic account of the life of Christ, and then I preached a Gospel message. The visit did alleviate some of Linda's fears, but neither Rick nor Linda were interested in church for themselves. They figured that was the end of that.

But Ray and Juanita kept right on praying. Occasionally Juanita gave them a Christian book (which they never read), or she suggested they should come to church (advice they never listened to). But they couldn't stop these godly Christians from praying.

Juanita went out soulwinning every Tuesday evening with another lady from our church, Joyce Jones. Each week, before Juanita and Joyce returned to the church, they drove out to the cul-de-sac where Rick and Linda lived. Several houses out of sight, they parked the car and prayed together for Rick and Linda's salvation. As J. Sidlow Baxter said, "Men may spurn our appeal, reject our message, oppose our arguments, despise our persons; but they are helpless against our prayers."

Gradually, through Ray and Juanita's testimony, Rick and Linda softened. They even showed up at church another Sunday morning. A few weeks later, they came again. Pretty soon, they were coming almost every week.

As the truth of the Gospel was beginning to penetrate their hearts, church began to get uncomfortable. Rick later explained that during the invitations at the end of the service, he would grip the pew in front of him to keep from yielding to the Holy Spirit's impulse to get saved.

Finally, during one invitation, Rick decided it wasn't worth resisting any longer. He grabbed Linda's hand, and together they went forward for salvation. Both were saved that day.

A FAITHFUL WITNESS

Just months after Rick and Linda's salvation, Juanita received the news that she had advanced cancer. Our entire church hurt for Juanita as the family shared the news with us.

Juanita was one of the sweetest Christian ladies I have ever known. Everyone who met Juanita, knew immediately that Juanita knew the Lord. She was a sweet, dedicated Christian lady, yielded to the Holy Spirit and full of His grace.

She was also one of the greatest soulwinners I have ever known. Once, during a major soulwinning campaign at our church, she came to me and asked for an extra map. "I'm retired now, so I have extra time," she explained. Over the next several weeks after her diagnosis, we all saw the depth of her passion for others.

Upon her diagnosis, Juanita was quickly admitted to the hospital, where she spent the next four weeks. Every single person who walked into Juanita's room whom she didn't already know—including nurses, doctors, and even a Jewish Rabbi—

received a Gospel tract. Even in her intense sickness, she cared for them and would ask, "Do you know the Lord?"

Juanita was discharged from the hospital into hospice care for the next three weeks. Through pain and heavy medication, she never lost her focus to lead people to the Lord. Each time a new hospice nurse came to care for her, she asked the same question she had asked hundreds of times in the hospital, "Do you know the Lord?"

Right up until her last moments, this Spirit-filled lady was fully engaged in leading others to a personal encounter with the Lord through a relationship with Christ.

Seven weeks after she learned she had cancer, Juanita went to be with the Lord. Linda said later, "During those seven weeks, she taught us more about faithfulness, soulwinning, and loving the Lord than we could have learned in years without her example."

It was through the life, prayers, and faithful witness of this godly lady that so many others, including her own family members, made the discovery of a lifetime—salvation. And through her influence, they have continued on a lifetime of discovery as they have grown in the Lord.

LEADING TO DISCOVERIES

This is the heart of ministry—leading others to a life-changing encounter with Christ through the cross.

But how does it happen? Authentic desert ministry is conducted in a way that reflects God's nature. It was primarily

Juanita's godly testimony that convinced Rick and Linda of the value of the Gospel.

We do not need to "trick" people into worshipping God through "marketing." We simply obey His command and lead people to Him through soulwinning.

The Apostle Paul recognized the value of the Gospel, and he made painstaking efforts to promote it with God-honoring motives and methods. In 1 Thessalonians 2:4 he explained, "But as we were allowed of God to be put in trust with the gospel, even so we speak; not as pleasing men, but God, which trieth our hearts."

Seeker-sensitive ministry has at its heart a desire to please men, and it appeals to men's fleshly natures to draw them. But God-honoring ministry recognizes that the ministry itself is a trust from God, and it magnifies *God's* nature in its means to promote the Gospel.

By our way of thinking, the first method would work better. And if the only goal is a crowd, it may work. But the second method, ministry that magnifies God's nature, works because God Himself empowers it, and it bears fruit in people's lives because it leads them to a genuine discovery of God.

FIRST ENCOUNTER

If you had asked eleventh grader Shonda Yarborough what her passion was, she would have told you cheerleading. Perhaps that's why she was so receptive when my daughter, Danielle, approached her cheerleading squad as they were preparing for practice at Highland High School.

Seeking to build a bridge, Danielle greeted the girls by saying, "I'm a cheerleader too!" Shonda connected immediately. Danielle gave each girl a flyer and invited them to come to a special teen rally our church was conducting the following week for our Open House Sunday. Shonda promised to come to the rally and gave Danielle her phone number.

That Saturday, Danielle called Shonda. "Hi, Shonda, this is Danielle from Lancaster Baptist Church. Just wanted to remind you about the teen rally at church tomorrow."

"Danielle!" Shonda answered enthusiastically. "Guess what? This guy named Jerry also invited my dad to your Open House. So my dad, my mom, and I are all coming tomorrow." Jerry Ferrso is one of our associate pastors, and he had made special efforts to invite public safety officials to the service. One of the men he met and invited was Shonda's dad, Mike, who worked at the prison.

Authentic desert ministry is conducted in a way that reflects God's nature.

What neither Jerry nor Danielle knew was that the Yarboroughs had actually been *looking* for a church. Mike and his wife, Brenda, had been saved years earlier. When they later moved to the Antelope Valley, they searched for a small church like the one they had been a part of in Sacramento, but they couldn't find one here with solid Bible preaching and teaching. They had given up their search about three years before this time. They were now willing to try a big church, however, and this double invitation to our church was welcomed.

Sure enough, that Sunday morning, Mike, Brenda, and Shonda came to church. Danielle met them when they arrived, and she walked with Shonda over to the teen rally in the other building.

At the close of the teen service, the preacher asked, "Do you know for sure you're on your way to Heaven?" Shonda was immediately interested, but she was too afraid to raise her hand. When Danielle leaned over and asked her if she would like to know more about what the preacher was talking about, she nodded her head, and Danielle had the privilege of leading her to Christ. Meanwhile, Mike and Brenda rededicated their lives to Christ. All three were baptized shortly afterward. The Yarborough's son, Greg, was also saved and baptized at Lancaster Baptist Church several months later.

DISCOVERING NEW DESTINIES

Throughout Shonda's senior year of high school, she carefully considered what she should do upon graduation. Through the mentoring of youth leaders, Shonda committed to attend West Coast Baptist College for one year. From there, she hoped to learn specifically what God had for her life.

Within a month into her freshman year, Shonda knew the Lord wanted her to graduate from West Coast Baptist College. During that year, she met Cody Kuehl, a young man who eventually asked her to marry him. Today, Cody and Shonda are serving together in Michigan, where Cody pastors a Baptist church.

Since that day when a courageous teenager invited a group of cheerleaders to church, the Yarborough's lives have been transformed. Not only are Shonda and Cody reaching many more lives through their church in Michigan, but Shonda's parents, Mike and Brenda, contribute to daily ministry at Lancaster Baptist Church. Mike is a godly deacon who serves the church family in many unseen ways. Brenda helps in a myriad of ministries, including teaching in the college, discipling new Christians, and doing volunteer proofreading. They are both faithful and fruitful soulwinners.

What the Yarborough family discovered during the morning of Open House Sunday changed their lives. More than attending church, they encountered God. And that is what desert ministry is all about.

THE GATE OF DISCOVERY

When God revealed Himself to Moses at the burning bush, Moses discovered God's power, and it transformed his life. But as Moses approached the bush, he made another discovery about God. It was a discovery that would give him a starting place to lead others into the presence of the Lord. In that encounter, Moses learned the defining attribute of God—holiness.

God's first instruction to Moses at the burning bush was "Draw not nigh hither: put off thy shoes from off thy feet, for the place whereon thou standest is holy ground" (Exodus 3:5).

Only the presence of God could transform ordinary hot sand into holy ground. And this transformation is what God has pledged to do today through the local church where the Bible is taught and Christ is honored. Jesus promised in Matthew 18:20, "For where two or three are gathered together in my name, there am I in the midst of them."

God's presence sets the church apart as a holy place, and He desires it to reflect its holy God.

WALKING ON HOLY GROUND

On that hot July day when we drove into Lancaster with all of our belongings in the Ryder truck behind us, we stopped first at the church, even before going to our apartment. Fully aware that we were embarking on a ministry of holy significance, I grabbed a screwdriver and hammer from the car and tore down the sign in front of the church displaying "Antelope Valley Church Center." Within days, I replaced the old sign with a new message—"Lancaster Baptist Church."

Only the presence of God could transform ordinary hot sand into holy ground.

Although we faced many unknowns concerning what might happen in this desert place, one thing was certain, this church belonged to God. It was "holy ground." While the previous sign might communicate a marketing philosophy, I wanted the community to know that the church was committed to proclaiming biblical truth and that it existed to honor Christ.

Of course, convincing the community of the biblical purpose of the church would require more than the change of a sign (although that was a good start). If the Lancaster

Baptist Church was to answer God's call to reach our valley with the Gospel, we would have to do more than recognize the holy ground. We must follow Moses' next action and remove our shoes.

God's command to Moses to remove his shoes signified the necessity of inner purity. The dusty shoes of desert travel represent the pollution of the world and the contamination of sin. We must lay these aside as we approach a holy God.

We can't walk on holy ground with polluted shoes. God has always called His people to a lifestyle of holiness. First Peter 1:16 expresses God's heart for His people, "Be ye holy; for I am holy." From the early days of Lancaster Baptist Church, it has been our desire that our lives individually and our church as a whole would reflect the holiness of our Lord.

EXALTING GOD'S HOLINESS

Much of today's Christianity trivializes the holiness of God. Charismatic leaders boast of special revelations of God, and television evangelists claim divine inspiration. But when Moses came face to face with a holy God, he "hid his face; for he was afraid to look upon God" (Exodus 3:6).

A genuine encounter with God leaves us speechless, not boastful. It reveals first our need for inner cleansing and then stirs our hearts for reverent worship.

We serve a God who displays His power in desert places, but if we are to know His presence and see His glory, we must recognize His holiness and approach Him in purity and reverence.

CONTINUALLY CONSUMED

Only a spectacular discovery could have arrested the attention of a seasoned, desert shepherd like Moses. The burning bush surprised him, but the discoveries He made about the nature of God consumed him and continued burning in his soul. In forty years of desert travel, Moses would discover the faithfulness of his God again and again.

The Mojave Desert looked so vast—so monotonous—when we first arrived. But the discoveries we've made here have transformed it to a place of immense beauty. God has revealed Himself to Lancaster Baptist Church as He has changed lives through the power of His Word and the ministry of the local church.

Ministry performed in the power of God's Spirit should not be mundane or lifeless. It should not be so routine that its barrenness is predictable. Authentic ministry should be consuming and full of constant discovery as we grow in our relationship with an infinite God. Our ministry and our worship should reflect Him. And in doing so, it will lead others to the greatest discoveries of their lives.

FOUR

DESERT PROVISION
WHEN FAITH MEETS NEEDS

I f this book were about likely people in likely places, the story I'm about to begin would go like this: Once there was a large church of wealthy people that was becoming larger. In fact, they were overflowing and desperately needed more space. The pastor presented the need to the people, and they all gave to build a new building. The end.

But the story of Lancaster Baptist Church is not quite so simple. Actually, our first building program started when our building was more empty than full. We were only a handful of people with no money, and few saw any need to expand.

When I came to Lancaster, our monthly mortgage payment for the church building was about $3,500.00. Our weekly offerings averaged $850.00. For the first year we received no salary as the church needed every penny of the offering to put toward the bills. (Our family was being supported by

43

other likeminded churches.) To help pay the mortgage, the church had been renting the main auditorium of the building to another church. Meanwhile, we met in a small, hot and stuffy upstairs classroom.

All week long, I visited homes in the community and invited people to church. Often, I'd be encouraged by a promised visit, only to be disappointed when the family didn't show on Sunday morning. Later that week, I'd visit again. The story was often the same, "We came, but there was a different pastor!" The visitors had mistakenly visited the downstairs church.

> *When God wants to perform a miracle, He always begins with a problem. The bigger the problem, the greater the miracle.*

I pointed out the dilemma to our people. Although we didn't have the money, we, by faith, asked the downstairs group to find a new location, and we assumed the entire payment of the building. Members gave sacrificially to meet mortgage payments, and the Lord blessed our church with steady numeric growth.

We moved to the downstairs main auditorium and roped off the back pews so our small congregation wouldn't be swallowed in the room that could seat several times the people we had.

It was in that mostly empty room that I told our church one Sunday evening, "We need to buy some property."

"What for?" one man blurted out, as he looked at the roped pews. "We're not even filling the building we have." Most people were too respectful to laugh out loud, but their faces betrayed the surprise and disbelief they were experiencing.

It was tough to explain. I just knew that God wanted to grow our church and that we needed to be ready for the expansion. This would be an opportunity for faith.

Although purchasing anything (especially land in a growing community) was a staggering proposition, we had two distinct assets: God and memory—the exact two assets the children of Israel neglected when they needed them the most.

A PROBLEM OF DIVINE PROPORTIONS

When God wants to perform a miracle, He always begins with a problem. The bigger the problem, the greater the miracle. We try to handle small problems on our own, without even looking to God. But mountainous problems—that's another story. We either give up or realize we need God. This is what I call a problem of divine proportions. It's so great that only God can solve it.

Exodus 16 is the record of such a problem. It is also the account of people who complained in unbelief rather than remembering they had a God who is a divine Problem Solver. It is the story of what God did in a desert place years ago for people who didn't deserve a miracle.

HUNGRY IN THE DESERT

The Israelites were approximately a month and a half into their desert journey to the Promised Land. Their food had run out, and they were hungry, tired, and grumbling. Like most of us, complaining was something the Israelites were very good at, so they set at it with expertise:

> And the whole congregation of the children of Israel murmured against Moses and Aaron in the wilderness: And the children of Israel said unto them, Would to God we had died by the hand of the LORD in the land of Egypt, when we sat by the flesh pots, and when we did eat bread to the full; for ye have brought us forth into this wilderness, to kill this whole assembly with hunger.—EXODUS 16:2–3

The Israelites truly were up against a serious problem— starvation. The barren wilderness through which they traveled could not sustain over two million people. Without a miracle they wouldn't make it.

BLINDED BY FLYING SAND

So, if the Israelites needed a miracle, why didn't they just ask God for one? These were people who had already seen God perform unprecedented wonders—the plagues of Egypt, the parting of the Red Sea, water from the rock, a pillar of fire and cloud to guide them. Surely the God who worked in these ways would provide food!

But the Israelites looked only at the present situation. They allowed the swirling desert sand to blind their vision.

That's how it always is. If we look at our circumstances alone, we complain and doubt God's care. But if we look at our circumstances through the eyes of faith in God, our approach is entirely different. You can either view the wilderness problems of divine proportions as wide receptacles for God's greatest miracles, or you can see only the dust and flying sand of negative circumstances. The difference in the vision is in your heart.

THE WAY-BACK-THEN SYNDROME

Do you notice something a little off in the Israelites' remembrance of Egypt? How could these ex-slaves rehearse their bondage as a time "when we sat by the flesh pots, and when we did eat bread to the full" (Exodus 16:3)? They were miserable in Egypt! They lived in "anguish of spirit" and "cruel bondage" (Exodus 6:9).

It seems that flying sand can bring on a serious malady—the "way-back-then syndrome." This disease distorts one's memory, skewing their perspective of the past. Victims remember only the positive parts of negative experiences.

I've seen Christians who, when going through a difficult season, look back to their lives before they were saved and remember only the pleasures of sin—not the consequences. They forget the emptiness and waste of those years, and they forget the goodness of God in their salvation and His willingness to intervene on their behalf today.

Others fall to this illness during a season of doubt after a step of faith. Perhaps they've given up a career or other opportunities to follow God's will. Now difficult circumstances have risen, and they remember only what they enjoyed before, forgetting the unrest of not fulfilling God's plan for their lives.

The way-back-then syndrome is a serious condition, but it can be remedied by wise use of one of God's greatest gifts memory.

THE BEST THINGS TO REMEMBER

Picture the contrast if the Israelites had chosen to remember God's goodness when hunger set in back in Exodus 16. Instead of complaining, they would have recalled God's recent miracles and anticipated yet another. They would have rehearsed to each other God's ability and willingness to provide.

God desires that we, His people, would use His past blessings to build our faith. When your mind is blurred by sandstorms of discouragement or doubt, purposefully recall God's past provision, and you will find the solid rock of faith. With a cleared perspective, you will see blessings of the past as evidence that God will work yet again.

I could fill several volumes with testimony to God's faithfulness to provide. One of my favorites happened in the earliest days of my ministry.

MIRACLE AT CABAZON

In the spring if 1980 I received a call slip to visit the vice president of the Bible College I was attending. When I arrived in his office, he shared with me that there were five or six ladies out in the lower desert past Palm Springs who had been praying that a church would be started in their area—Coachella, California. He asked me if I would be interested in driving out to Coachella on the following Sunday. As a young man called to preach the Gospel, this was exciting news indeed! A few days later, I took a small group of students from the college, and we drove 150 miles one way to preach to five precious ladies.

That morning I preached a message for which I had studied and prepared for several hours. It was about God's grace in remembering Noah. I preached about Noah's righteousness and the antediluvian society's wickedness. I described the animals entering the ark. I expounded on the ark being a picture of Christ's salvation. I preached everything I knew about Noah and the ark, and the entire sermon lasted eight minutes!

Much to my surprise, those ladies asked me if I would come back and preach the following week.

God desires that we would use His past blessings to build our faith.

I gladly consented, and for the next three years I spent every Saturday and Sunday ministering to a small town of about two thousand and establishing a Bible-believing Baptist church.

Terrie and I were married in December 1980, and we traveled together from the Los Angeles area where we attended Bible College to the lower desert where I preached each weekend. When our baby girl, Danielle, was born a couple of years later, we felt it was time to purchase a car with reliable air conditioning. Sometimes the temperatures reached well above 110 degrees Fahrenheit. Danielle was often in the back seat drenched in perspiration all the way home from Coachella. We went to a "fine Christian automobile dealer" who sold us a 1970s model orange Honda hatchback station wagon. It wasn't much to look at, but we were sure thankful for the air conditioning.

Our first trip out to the desert in our new car felt like a journey of luxury, and we enjoyed the air conditioning all the way. As we headed home that evening, I noticed the air conditioning did not seem very cool. In fact, it had completely stopped working. Once again, we rolled down the windows, and our bodies began to perspire against the vinyl seats.

As we merged onto Interstate 10 for the last ninety miles of our trip, our car began sputtering and losing power. Looking up to the horizon, I saw the two unusual landmarks that identified an area known as Cabazon. Two large concrete dinosaurs towered above the surrounding desert. I estimated that they were two or three miles in the distance. Just then, the car gave a final sputter and completely lost power. I steered to the shoulder of the road and turned on the emergency flashers.

I got out of the car, opened the hood, looked at the engine, and acted as though I knew what I was doing. After I looked under the hood, I did what all men do who wish they knew what they were looking for. I walked around the car, kicked the tires, and looked again at the engine. The fact was, I knew nothing about Honda hatchback station wagons, and I certainly had no idea why the car had stopped running.

Soon, Danielle started crying. Her curly blonde hair was wet with sweat, and tears were running down her cheeks. Terrie's eyes were full of tears as well, and I was contemplating the fact that we would need to walk two or three miles to the Cabazon gas station.

Every Sunday morning before we left home and every Sunday afternoon as we began our return trip, we paused to ask

God for safety and wisdom in our travels. This day, however, as we were stranded in the desert, it seemed as if there were no answers for the prayers we had made.

As I prepared for the walk to Cabazon, I noticed an elderly couple in a brand new Cadillac had pulled over just behind us. The gentleman got out of his car and greeted me, "Hello, Pastor Paul. It looks like you need some help today."

I had no idea who he was, but I definitely knew I needed help. Within moments, he had helped me, Terrie, and Danielle into his beautifully air conditioned Cadillac. The couple drove us to the Cabazon gas station. Adjacent to the station was the Hadley fruit stand and restaurant. The gentleman parked his car and took us into the restaurant. As we sat down, he said, "Just one moment, and I'll be right back." Terrie and I ordered some soft drinks and waited for the gentleman and his wife, whom we assumed would come in and join us for a quick meal.

A few moments later, he returned. "I have spoken to the men who run the garage next door, he explained. "They have sent a tow truck to pick up your car. I have given them my credit card number and told them to charge any repairs to my account." He shook my hand and said, "Never stop preaching the Gospel." With that, he turned away and went back to the car where his wife was waiting.

The entire moment had caught Terrie and me by surprise. I looked in my hand and saw a one hundred dollar bill. Within the matter of a few hours, we had a wonderful meal, a new part in our car, one hundred dollars placed in my hand, and an admonition from a man whom we often have thought may have been an angel sent from Heaven to encourage us in the ministry.

There has never been a week since that evening twenty-eight years ago that we have not given of ourselves to spread the Gospel of Jesus Christ. During difficult days, the Lord often reminds me of the grace He bestowed upon us in a little desert town marked with two dinosaurs on Interstate 10. As I remember God's provision, I'm encouraged to trust Him further.

A MIRACLE OF MERCY

The first miracle God showed the Israelites when they complained of hunger was not the manna. It was mercy.

I don't know about you, but griping turns me off. (At least other people's griping; I'm usually fine with my own!) Israel's complaints were particularly grievous because they were an assault on God's character. They showed no confidence, trust, or gratitude toward the God who had delivered them from slavery and brought them safely thus far. When they said, "Would to God we had died by the hand of the LORD in the land of Egypt" (Exodus 16:3), they were questioning God's goodness and wisdom.

Their words mirror the thoughts Satan sometimes tries to put into our minds: "If God is so good, why did He let me lose my home, my job, my health…?" Yet God is merciful, and in His kindness, He delivers rather than destroys. Lamentations 3:22–23 highlights His goodness: "It is of the LORD's mercies that we are not consumed, because his compassions fail not. They are new every morning: great is thy faithfulness."

Thank God for the miracle of His mercy! Far from responding in exasperation, God did the extraordinary.

EXTRAORDINARY DESERT PROVISION

Leave it to me to come up with food for two million people in the desert, and they would probably be eating Spam (delivered by a camel caravan). It's cheap and simple. But God's solutions to our problems are as creative as they are great. He actually *rained bread*. Who but God would have even *thought* of the plan, let alone had the ability to perform it?

Psalm 78:25 refers to the manna delicacy as "angels' food." God doesn't scrimp for His children. He doesn't have to—He's God. And He is as extravagant as He is merciful.

When we face problems of divine proportions, God invites, "Call unto me," and He promises, "I will answer thee, and shew thee great and mighty things, *which thou knowest not*" (Jeremiah 33:3, emphasis added). He has better answers to our problems than we even know to ask for.

PROOF OR FAITH

Can you imagine standing in Moses' place in the desert and telling the Israelites that God was going to provide enough food that they could eat until they were filled? This would require at least three hundred boxcar loads of bread! And at that moment, the people were standing in the middle of a barren desert—no food in sight.

The people could have replied, "Prove it. We'll believe it when we see it." But Moses didn't have proof. He only had faith. And the difference between the two changes one's entire approach to problems of divine proportions. In short, proof doubts; faith expects.

Moses surely didn't have any greater understanding of how God was going to perform this miracle than the people did. But because he remembered what God did in the past, he could boldly tell the people that God would in fact provide for them. That's another difference between doubt and faith—doubt forgets; faith remembers.

When I stood in our mostly empty auditorium that Sunday evening in 1987 and told our people that we needed to purchase property to grow, I couldn't understand how God was going to work things out. But our church chose to follow the faith that God had placed in my heart, and a few weeks later we had our first building banquet, with the theme "Giving by Faith."

A NIGHT TO BE REMEMBERED

I'll never forget that banquet night. I doubt anyone else who was there will forget it either.

It started as a nightmare. We had inadvertently hired the world's most dysfunctional catering company. They delivered the food late, and then their ineffectively designed food lines required hours to serve the food. Our church pianist must have played every song she knew a dozen times before everyone was served.

Between the stress of overseeing an unmanageable event and wondering how this confusion could ever result in new property, I began to doubt. Satan pointed out some of the new Christians gathered. "Why," he whispered, "are you asking them to give above the tithe for a project you don't understand when they haven't even started *tithing*?"

Then Satan directed my attention to the man who occasionally attended, always wearing his cap. For some reason, this gentleman refused to remove his cap unless I personally asked him. This night was no different. I saw him enter and quietly went to him. "Would you mind taking your cap off in church?" "Alright," he grumbled loudly, "but only for you, Preacher." Satan persisted, "This guy doesn't even know how to take off his hat in church, and you're asking him to give to an unspecified project?"

Satan pointed to the few families there who had lost their jobs the week before, and he reminded me of their discouragement. Just days before they had told me, "We don't see how we can even make it. Don't expect us to be able to give anything at the banquet."

As I surveyed the people in the room—half of whom were still waiting for their meal, I wondered how God was going to provide. This was not looking good. And yet, when we passed the plate, the unbelievable evening of mishap turned to an unbelievable moment of faith. *Fifty thousand dollars* was given that night by just a handful of families.

Several days later, I drove by a large piece of corner property for sale. I wrote down the number on the sign and hurried home to call the realtor. When I explained on the phone who I was and what church I was from, the realtor assured me that this was not the property for us—too expensive. "You'd need $50,000 just to put it into escrow."

Long story short, we own the property today, plus some. To the glory of God, several multi-million dollar buildings have sprouted across our eighty-acre campus as monuments to the desert provision of God.

Ever since that first building banquet we seem to be in an ongoing building program. We need space, we build, we grow, and then we need to expand further. But each time we face facility needs, our people can look around the property and buildings God has provided in the desert and remember God's past provision. We trust and serve a great God, and we have good reason to remember His incredible works of the past.

OPPORTUNITIES EXTRAORDINAIRE

Are you facing a problem of divine proportions? Then you have an extraordinary opportunity to see miraculous desert provision! Desert needs are really desert opportunities, disguised.

Listen to Moses' encouragement: "In the morning, then ye shall see the glory of the LORD" (Exodus 16:7). You may face a desert need today, but God will provide.

It's hard to see God's glory when you're blinded by flying sand or languishing with the "way-back-then syndrome." Choose instead to remember the greatness of our God. Meet desert needs with faith—faith that expects and faith that remembers. Seize the opportunity to see the glory of God.

You don't have to just *live* in the desert. You can see God's glory in the desert.

FIVE

DESERT WITNESS
WHERE FRUIT ABOUNDS

Bill Anderson is the kind of man every pastor appreciates. I remember when Bill and his wife, Cori, first visited Lancaster Baptist Church. Bill was stationed at Edwards Air Force Base, about thirty miles from our church. The Anderson family quickly became involved in their adult Bible class, and Cori jumped in to help with the deaf ministry. Both eagerly learned how to lead others to the Lord and became faithful soulwinners. As they continued to grow in grace, God knit the Andersons' hearts to our church and our hearts to theirs.

A few years later, we were all saddened when Bill was transferred to Incirlik, Turkey. I prayed diligently for Bill, as there was no church like ours near the base in Turkey. None of us foresaw, however, the exciting chain of events that Bill was soon to be a part of.

DRAMA IN THE DESERT

Desert drama is fascinating. For one thing, it's usually a surprise. It's not that the desert is boring—it isn't. But neither is it the place that you expect to be the scene of miracles. It's just...out of the way, sort of private. By my way of thinking, if God was going to perform a miracle, surely He would choose a large metropolis, not the backside of the desert!

Another reason desert drama is intriguing is because it requires a unique cast and plot. Since the desert doesn't generate its own drama, the plot must be specially crafted, and it usually has a surprise ending.

Such is the drama of Acts 8. Before we see this captivating story unfold, let's go backstage and meet the cast.

A MAN WITH A MESSAGE

We meet the first character of this drama in Acts 6. Philip was a faithful man in the church at Jerusalem whose servant leadership was noticed by the entire church. When the church selected the first deacons, he was among the seven chosen. He must have been a man of sterling character and compassionate generosity.

It wasn't long, however, before the Jerusalem church faced serious testing. The Pharisees were insanely envious of Christianity's growth. Every day, more Jews were trusting Christ as their Messiah and numbering themselves among the Christians. Persecution by the Pharisees soon followed, and many Christians fled Jerusalem to escape.

Philip was among those who left Jerusalem, and, like so many of the others, he was faithful to preach the Gospel everywhere he went. Thus, the persecution that the Pharisees intended as a tool to stamp out Christianity actually helped to spread it.

Philip made a special trip into Samaria—a region greatly despised by the Jews. He preached the Gospel, and so many people trusted Christ that Acts 8:8 comments, "…there was great joy in that city."

Scripture doesn't tell us Philip's primary occupation, but we know that he was occupied with the message of salvation. Philip was a man with a message, and everywhere he went, he couldn't help but share his message.

A WITNESS IN TURKEY

Bill Anderson is sort of a reserved guy. But he is a man with a message. So when he found himself at Incirlik Air Force Base in Turkey, he decided to get out his message via the base bulletin board. He tacked up a card that read: "Wanted: a few good men to pray with."

It was that simple announcement, nestled into a full bulletin board in a foreign country, that enlisted Bill in a drama he could have never written.

Bill could have reasoned, "I don't need to be a witness here. I'm only here for the US Air Force. Besides, I'm shy, and these guys will just make fun of me." But Bill wasn't content to just work on aircraft. He had a message that he felt compelled to tell.

This is God's intent for every one of His children. Whatever your official job description may be, make sharing the Gospel your mission in life. Some of the greatest soulwinners I know are men and women who see spreading the message of the Gospel as their chief mission. Their actual occupations vary—engineers, soldiers, businessmen, pharmacists, housewives, doctors, janitors—a full spectrum. But their passion is the same—to deliver the message of the Gospel.

CALLED ON STAGE

Philip's Gospel message in Samaria was so well received that when the church at Jerusalem heard the news, they decided to send Peter and John to disciple the new converts. Surely these were some of the most exciting and fulfilling days of Philip's life.

And yet, God called Philip *away* from the action: "And the angel of the Lord spake unto Philip, saying, Arise, and go toward the south unto the way that goeth down from Jerusalem unto Gaza, which is desert" (Acts 8:26). There it is again—a desert place. An unlikely place. A place not of Philip's choosing.

If I were in Philip's shoes, I think I would have been inclined to second-guess this call. Perhaps I didn't hear clearly. Perhaps this was just a whim. How could it be God's will to leave fruitful ministry and head to the desert?

But I think we see a pattern by now. When God calls His people to desert places, He performs wonders. Sometimes the stage on which He is going to perform a miracle is out of the way, in the lonely desert.

THE STAGE SET

Sure of God's voice, Philip began his anticlimactic journey toward Gaza on what is now called the Via Maris trade route.

Let's take a look at this desert stage. Gaza was one of five Philistine cities. It was a rough place, a needy place. It's not the sort of place most men would choose to build a church.

We have cities similar in spiritual dearth today, and most of them have few or no Baptist churches. Within three hundred miles of Lancaster, there are several desperately needy cities— Hollywood, Las Vegas, even Los Angeles have only a few Gospel preaching churches. These are cities well-known for their spiritual darkness, but who is bringing them light?

I pray today for men who will listen for God's call to come to these cities. I believe these cities could be the scenes of God's greatest miracles. But I fear we are sometimes too soft to go to the desert.

David Livingstone knew what it was to bring the Gospel to hard places. For thirty years, he poured his life into bringing the Gospel to the people of Africa. A missionary society once wrote Livingstone offering to send help: "Have you found a good road to where you are? If so, we want to know how to send other men to join you." Livingstone wrote back, "If you have men who will come only if they know there is a good road, I don't want them. I want men who will come if there is no road at all."

Livingstone's statement reveals the heart of a man with a message who is willing to go anywhere—even the hard places— to deliver the message. This is the spirit that builds great churches. This was the spirit of Philip—"I'll leave my ministry and go to the desert."

And thus Philip found himself on the stage of a desert drama.

A MAN WHO IS SEARCHING

Let's move back off-stage for a moment and meet another cast member. He also is traveling the Via Maris. He is seated in a chariot, escorted by a large party. This is a man of great importance—Treasurer to the Queen of Ethiopia.

But why would this Ethiopian be out near Gaza? We can see by the direction of his chariot that he was homeward bound. In fact, he was returning from a trip to Jerusalem. Since Ethiopia is at least five hundred miles from Jerusalem, this must have been a significantly important journey.

Perhaps the scroll in his hands will give us a clue to his purpose. Indeed! It's the book of Isaiah. This must be a man searching for the truth. Despite his power and prestige, he had a vast emptiness in his soul. He was returning from a long, arduous journey, still searching for the true God.

THE CURTAIN LIFTS

The stage is now set, and the actors are in place to enter at precisely the same moment—only neither of them knows of the other. Right there, in the middle of the desert, God lifts the curtain for a spectacular desert meeting.

As Philip trudges along, he sees the Ethiopian's chariot. "Then the Spirit said unto Philip, Go near, and join thyself to this chariot. And Philip ran thither to him, and heard him read the prophet Esaias, and said, Understandest thou what thou readest? And he said, How can I, except some man should guide me? And he desired Philip that he would come up and sit with him" (Acts 8:29–31).

Philip, the man with a message, gladly joined the Ethiopian, the man who was searching. Philip shared his message, and the Ethiopian found his answer—Jesus.

> *The place of the scripture which he read was this, He was led as a sheep to the slaughter; and like a lamb dumb before his shearer, so opened he not his mouth: In his humiliation his judgment was taken away: and who shall declare his generation? for his life is taken from the earth.*
>
> *And the eunuch answered Philip, and said, I pray thee, of whom speaketh the prophet this? of himself, or of some other man? Then Philip opened his mouth, and began at the same scripture, and preached unto him Jesus.*
>
> *And as they went on their way, they came unto a certain water: and the eunuch said, See, here is water; what doth hinder me to be baptized? And Philip said, If thou believest with all thine heart, thou mayest. And he answered and said, I believe that Jesus Christ is the Son of God. And he commanded the chariot to stand still: and they went down both into the water, both Philip*

and the eunuch; and he baptized him. And when they were come up out of the water, the Spirit of the Lord caught away Philip, that the eunuch saw him no more: and he went on his way rejoicing.—ACTS 8:32–39

The events in this drama are a soulwinner's dream: to have someone actually ask you to explain the Gospel. It's a script that only God could put together.

THE SCRIPTWRITER

We've already seen the backgrounds of Philip and the Ethiopian. But what do we learn of the Scriptwriter through this masterpiece?

The fact that God included the Ethiopian in this desert drama—in fact, wrote the script for his salvation—tells us something about God: He sees those searching for the truth and sends a soulwinner. Luke 19:10 says, "For the Son of man is come to seek and to save that which was lost."

Matching searching people with Spirit-filled soulwinners is the Lord of the harvest's specialty. Although I have never experienced someone specifically asking me, "What must I do to be saved?" I've often had the privilege of leading people to the Lord whose hearts God had already prepared for our meeting. Sometimes I encounter these prepared hearts while making scheduled visits or while going doorknocking. Other times, however, these are people with whom the Lord crosses my path in daily business and prompts me to witness.

One of the most exciting parts of ministry in the desert is seeing God use you to bring the Gospel to a searching heart.

MAKING THE AUDITION

Would you like to be part of a desert drama like this? It's a simple audition.

It would seem that God would choose people for parts like Philip's based on talent, experience, or skill. But if there's anything we've learned so far about God's work in desert places, it's that God doesn't make His selections on natural gifting. (Remember Moses?)

First Corinthians 1:26–28 are encouraging words for those of us who know we don't have ability apart from God: "For ye see your calling, brethren, how that not many wise men after the flesh, not many mighty, not many noble, are called: But God hath chosen the foolish things of the world to confound the wise; and God hath chosen the weak things of the world to confound the things which are mighty; And base things of the world, and things which are despised, hath God chosen, yea, and things which are not, to bring to nought things that are."

So, if God doesn't choose people for their natural gifts, does this make God's selections arbitrary? Not at all!

Notice a particular quality—one that any of us can learn— which specifically fitted Philip for his role: Philip was obedient.

Have you ever tried to direct a cast who wouldn't follow directions? Even the best director can't do much with cast members who ignore him or refuse to submit to him. And so it is with the Lord. When we ignore His promptings or refuse to submit to His leadership, we forfeit the opportunity to be part of desert drama. If, however, we'll obey every prompting of the Holy Spirit, we'll have the opportunity to live out the incredible scripts He writes for our lives. It's that simple.

SIMPLE BUT DIFFICULT

Although obedience is simple, it's not always easy. It couldn't have been easy for Philip to leave the revival in Samaria to go to the desert! But Acts 8:27 says simply, "And he arose and went." No questions, no delay—he just obeyed.

When God called our family to Lancaster, we faced a simple decision—obey God and go, or disobey and stay. Although the decision was simple, the move was difficult. We were on staff in a growing ministry, and there was no salary in Lancaster. (There wasn't even enough to keep the church budget afloat!) We had friends and security where we were. In Lancaster, we knew no one.

We could have delayed, waiting until we found answers for the tough questions, but we would have missed getting to be involved in a desert drama far better than I could have ever imagined! I'm glad we obeyed.

TRUST THE DIRECTOR'S CUES

When God sent Philip to the desert, Philip had no idea why God was directing him there. He didn't even know what he was going to do when he arrived. But he understood God's immediate instruction, and he started walking.

Once in the desert, Philip had another opportunity to obey. God told him to join himself to the chariot—to run up to a moving chariot and start talking to the passenger, a man he had never met. Philip had no idea that the Ethiopian was reading Isaiah and was ready to hear the Gospel. He just trusted the director's cues and immediately obeyed. God did the rest.

I wonder how many desert dramas we miss, simply because we don't trust the Director's cues. How many times has the Holy Spirit prompted and we *didn't* obey? Fear of what we'll look like or how we'll be perceived or if we'll be rejected holds us back.

All of us would be willing to witness to someone if we knew ahead of time that they would get saved. But here's the catch—we never know what will happen until we obey.

This basic obedience is the bottom line to being Spirit-filled. It boils down to being sensitive to hear the voice of God and then immediately obeying every impulse of the Holy Spirit. True desert ministry happens when Spirit-filled soulwinners encounter people whose hearts God has been preparing for the Gospel.

BILL'S OPPORTUNITY FOR DRAMA

It wasn't long after Bill tacked his announcement to the bulletin board that he started receiving calls. Soon, he was hosting a few families in his home every week for a Bible study. They sang hymns and played some of my sermons on tapes. The Lord used these meetings to bring spiritual encouragement and support to Bill and the other people who met with him. Before Bill left

Turkey, this group had grown to over two hundred people meeting every Sunday.

But Bill's ministry did not stop with the American military. God gave Bill an unusual rapport with the Turkish people. Because there was no available housing on base, Bill rented a small house near a Turkish village. The village people were delighted! Bill was the first American to live near their village, and to show their appreciation, they gave him a cow and chickens. Bill's landlord's wife even milked the cow for him and brought him fresh milk each morning.

True desert ministry happens when Spirit-filled soulwinners encounter people whose hearts God has been preparing for the Gospel.

Bill's Turkish neighbors noticed the Bible studies at his home and started asking him questions. Before long, he led the owner of a local tavern to Christ. The man, Yassin, was serious about following Christ and shut down his tavern. He even asked Bill to turn it into a church.

During Bill's seventeen months in Turkey, several Turkish families were saved and met together in the converted tavern. After Bill returned to the States, these families continued meeting to study and grow in God's Word. As they told their Muslim families of their decision to follow Christ, they were making an incredibly significant step of commitment. Persecution soon followed.

Turkish law permits individuals to be Christian, but it forbids Christians to proselyte or to own property. And Turkish culture ostracizes those who turn from Islam. Yassin and the group of young Christians meeting in his ex-tavern soon felt the brunt of persecution. They lost their jobs and homes and moved out into the fields and mountains. Like the first-century Jerusalem Christians, many of them fled the area.

In the process of their move, Bill lost track of Yassin. It looked like this was the end of an incredible drama that Bill had never expected. But, as Bill later learned, this was only the close of the first scene.

A NEW STAGE—IN THE DESERT

About eight years later, Bill was again sent overseas, this time as a civilian contractor in Baghdad. About a month after getting settled into his new routine, he had the most surprising meeting of his life.

"Abi Billy!"

Bill hadn't been addressed in this endearing term of respect for years, especially not in the unmistakable accent he had just heard. He swung around, and there, standing in front of him, was Yassin.

The men hugged, and Yassin brought Bill up to date on his life. When he fled Incirlik, he moved to Northern Turkey. There he worked as a shopkeeper near another military base. Later, he got a job with the US government, which eventually brought him to Baghdad.

Bill was thrilled to see Yassin, and he was encouraged to see that he still loved the Lord and was eager to talk of Him. The two men spent the rest of the day fellowshipping in a nearby Turkish restaurant.

The following morning, Bill received the sad news that Yassin had just been killed in a terrorist attack.

That afternoon, Bill heard a heavy knock on his door. He opened the door to see two huge Turks standing on his doorstep. "Are you Bill?" they asked. "We want to know what Yassin has." Yassin had tried witnessing to these men before, but they didn't listen. Now, they knew Yassin had known the truth.

Bill once again told hungry Turkish hearts the sweet story of Christ's love. Both men were saved that afternoon.

EPILOGUE

After Philip led the Ethiopian to Christ, the Holy Spirit separated their paths. The Ethiopian continued on his way, but Philip was "caught away" to Azotus. Acts 8:39 says of the Ethiopian, "and he went on his way rejoicing." I think it is safe to say that Philip was also rejoicing! No doubt, the Ethiopian saw many come to Christ as he returned to his home country and with joy shared the Gospel he had just received.

Bill and Yassin have likewise experienced the joy that comes through involvement in the Holy Spirit's scripts. Yassin is rejoicing in the very presence of the Lord. Bill is back in the States, and the Andersons are faithful members of Lancaster Baptist Church. Bill is overwhelmed and thankful for spiritual fruit God gave him in Turkey and Iraq. And knowing that Yassin is already with the Lord, makes him even more grateful to have had a part in his salvation.

FRUIT IN THE DESERT

Ministry can happen in the desert—in the out-of-the-way places—by the Spirit of God. Who would have expected the first Ethiopian convert to be a man of prestige traveling through the middle of nowhere? Who would have expected a Turkish tavern owner to trust Christ, convert his tavern to a church, and then show up in the desert of Iraq, still bearing spiritual fruit? Who would have expected God to raise up a thriving church in the Mojave Desert? Who would have expected God to use this church to touch lives in the desert and transform them by His grace?

Some of my dearest friends labor in the out-of-the-way places—not necessarily literal deserts, but insignificant places. Yet, one by one, their ministries are touching lives with the power of the Gospel.

Perhaps you see your sphere of influence as an insignificant place. You're the only Christian at your workplace. Your church is small. Your voice is unheard. You live and minister in a desert.

Remember, the Holy Spirit can bring fruit even in the desert. He's given us all a message. Simply trust His cues, deliver His message, and watch Him unfold a drama of desert fruitfulness.

SIX

DESERT GUIDANCE
WHEN ADVERSITY BLOWS

A brief look of concern clouded the radiant admiration in Nikki's eyes as she gazed at her one-day-old baby girl. Was it just the lighting, or was baby Lydia's skin actually yellow?

Scott and Nikki Hand were a young couple in our church in 1998 when Lydia was born. Nikki's dad, Ed Marquez, was one of our deacons, and her mom, Sherry, served as a church secretary. The entire family was so excited about Scott and Nikki's first baby. But this family was soon to face an intense storm of unforeseen proportions.

The Hands brought Lydia to the doctor to ask about the yellow tone in her skin. He said it was just jaundice, something babies get sometimes when their bilirubin count rises higher than normal. He prescribed that Lydia spend three days back in the hospital under special lights. But the yellow didn't go away.

A specialist at the children's hospital in Los Angeles ran a battery of tests and made a different diagnoses—biliary atresia. Jaundice is only a symptom of this life-threatening disease in which a baby's liver cells are destroyed and replaced by scar tissue. This is the result of improperly developed liver ducts that do not allow the liver's bile to excrete properly. The doctor recommended a procedure that would remove Lydia's damaged liver ducts and replace them with a length of her intestine.

God's love is predictable— unchangeable, unmovable, unshakable.

At two months old, Lydia underwent this five-hour surgery. She remained in the hospital for a week, and the family's hope soared high. Once again, Scott and Nikki brought their little one home from the hospital, this time praying she would be healthy.

Within two months, however, the doctor examined a deeply yellow-skinned Lydia and confirmed the apparent—the surgery had not cured the problem. He recommended they place Lydia on the list for a liver transplant and pray a donor would soon become available. Lydia wouldn't be able to survive much longer without a functioning liver.

At five months, Lydia was hospitalized. She weighed less than ten pounds and hardly had the energy to fuss. Her digestive system couldn't work properly without a liver, so she had to be fed intravenously. Her tiny tummy swelled with fluids, and she had emergency surgeries and blood transfusions for internal bleeding.

Lydia was fading by the hour. A few months earlier, Scott had told the doctor, "We'll do anything to make our little girl healthy." And he meant it. But there was nothing they could do—just watch her suffer. As a pastor, it was heartbreaking to watch this young couple as the dark storm clouds moved ominously closer.

Scott's mom flew in from Georgia and joined Scott and Nikki in their room at the Ronald McDonald house across the street from the hospital. Ed and Sherry drove the almost 150-mile round trip from Lancaster daily. Terrie and I made many trips to the children's hospital ourselves. All of us spent hours in fervent prayer for Lydia, who was quickly slipping away. In the midst of the raging storm, we all anchored our hope to the unchanging promises of God's Word.

STORMS IN THE DESERT

Desert storms can be violent. Racing winds and flash floods threaten the survival of anyone unsheltered or unprotected.

I'll never forget the storm I encountered on my way out to Edwards Air Force Base for a soulwinning call several years ago. Stronger than usual gales of wind hurled tumbleweeds across the desert, and lightning struck the ground in the distance. I briefly wondered if I should wait for another day to make the drive, but I decided against it.

As I drove out of town, the wind grew stronger. Billowing sand greatly reduced visibility, and I struggled to see the road. It was as if I were driving in a brown blizzard. The taillights of the car in front of me veered to the right as the driver pulled off the road. Again, I considered turning back but instead pressed on.

When an upward thrust of wind briefly lifted the sand cloud, I took the moment to regain my bearings and make a low panoramic sweep. Already, two cars had collided at a nearby intersection. The wind struck again, and I gripped the steering wheel to stay on the road. A minute later, the wind once again restored visibility. This time I looked up—just in time to see the telephone pole in front of me snap. I jerked the transmission into reverse and backed out just as the pole fell where my car had been.

My determination to make it out to the base dissipated. I turned the car around and headed home, just as the downpour started. All the way, I watched telephone poles snap like toothpicks as the rain poured in torrents.

STORMS OF THE SOUL

The storms that come into our lives are often similar in their intensity to the storms that sweep the desert. Sickness, criticism, financial instability, disappointment, and any number of other factors come upon us in a downpour.

And yet, the God who works miracles in desert places can also guide His people safely through the desert storms.

The Israelites are a classic case study. They spent forty years in what Moses described as a "waste howling wilderness"

(Deuteronomy 32:10). At the end of this journey, Moses recorded a song of praise summing up God's care for His people. Deuteronomy 32:7–14 reveals God's heart for those in desert storms, and it highlights God's faithful guidance for us as we also navigate the "howling wildernesses" of life.

SECURITY FOR THE SOUL

If there's anything you long for in a storm, it's security. Storms in the desert often rise unexpectedly, and they rage unpredictably. Things that once seemed so secure and solid, crash and cave in around you, and you wonder what will tumble next.

For the Christian, there is a place of security in storms of the soul, and it is the all-encompassing love of God. God's love is predictable. It's unchangeable, unmovable, unshakable. It remains a bedrock of hope, and we can survive any desert storm from its shelter.

In Moses' song of praise, he emphasized God's love in pointing out that God actually *chose* Israel for Himself: "For the LORD's portion is his people; Jacob is the lot of his inheritance" (Deuteronomy 32:9). God, as the Creator of the universe, could choose anything for Himself. Yet, He chose Israel for His portion.

The cross of Christ emphasizes another choice of God's love—me and you. "For God so loved the world, that he gave his only begotten Son..." (John 3:16). God chose to love me, even when that choice cost Him everything. Because of the redemption of Christ, we who have trusted in Him are His people and His portion. We belong to Him.

> *But ye are a chosen generation, a royal priesthood, an*
> *holy nation, a peculiar people; that ye should shew forth*
> *the praises of him who hath called you out of darkness*
> *into his marvellous light; Which in time past were not*
> *a people, but are now the people of God: which had*
> *not obtained mercy, but now have obtained mercy.*
> —1 PETER 2:9–10

Let the storm rage. God's love reaches the deepest desert crevices and secures His people in its shelter.

ASSAULT ON THE SHELTER

Not surprisingly, God's love is often Satan's first target during desert storms. He relentlessly bombards our minds with doubt and assaults our souls with fear. "How could this be happening to you if God loves you?" he questions. Or he torments our mind with the nagging "why?" He implies that we have to understand *why* God is allowing the storm before we can believe His love.

Lydia's grandmother, Sherry, related the temptation to question God's love during the storm. "It truly was a struggle for me," she acknowledged. "There were people throwing their babies in dumpsters, and we even heard one report of a lady out walking her dogs who found a live baby who had been tossed into a grave in a park. I'd look at Scott and Nikki who wanted and dearly loved their baby and wonder, *Why them? Why is this happening?*"

Sherry said it was the strength of God's Word that upheld her through the storm. "Had it not been for Proverbs 3:5–6, who knows where I would have been. But these verses helped me know that I didn't have to understand why this was happening; I just needed to trust the Lord. Every time my mind would begin to struggle, I'd go back to these verses. It was God's Word that got us through."

STAY IN THE SHELTER

More people die in the desert each year of drowning than of dehydration. Everyone expects dearth in the desert, so they find or develop water sources. But flash floods descend suddenly and claim many unprepared lives.

We have the life-giving stream of God's Word available constantly, and it provides written assurance of God's unchanging love. Reading it and believing it helps us rest in the shelter of God's protection during the storm. But when we neglect to trust its promises, we make ourselves vulnerable to the floods of doubt that rage just outside our shelter.

When every circumstance surrounding you and every feeling within you seems to contradict God's love, believe it anyway. Drink from the promises of God's Word and trust His love.

SUPPORT IN THE STORM

Moses summed up forty years of God's provision in three phrases: "he led him about, he instructed him, he kept him as the apple of his eye" (Deuteronomy 32:10b).

How revealing of God's heart for people in desert places! He leads us, teaches us, and keeps us, especially through the storms.

For forty years, God led Israel faithfully. He knew and provided for their needs—manna, quail, water, protection—one miracle after another. Rest assured, the same God will lead you through your desert storm if you will simply trust His guidance.

Probably the two greatest lessons the Lord taught the Israelites in the desert were to keep Him preeminent and to trust Him. In the midst of a storm, our tendency is to look desperately for solutions, to just do something, anything. But when we keep our eyes on the Lord and make Him our first priority, it becomes much easier to rest in His love.

CABIN FEVER

The urge to just "do something" during a desert storm is strong. And when we realize we can't do anything about the present situation, sometimes we demand that *God* just "do something." We're tired of residing in the shelter of His love when it seems our life is caving in around us. Like a camper with cabin fever, we just want out. We want to run—to escape.

But to experience the security of God's shelter, we must be still and allow Him to teach us. In Psalm 32:8–9, He pleads, "I will instruct thee and teach thee in the way which thou shalt go: I will guide thee with mine eye. Be ye not as the horse, or as the mule, which have no understanding: whose mouth must be held in with bit and bridle, lest they come near unto thee."

Our cabin fever frustration is often the result of being like the horse or mule described in these verses who stubbornly insists on its own way. Instead of allowing the Lord to lead us, we want to push ahead, creating our own answers. God will lead us and teach us if we will wait on Him.

DESERT PROTECTION

Desert storms have a way of making you feel desolate—isolated and even forsaken. The whipping wind sweeps unstopped across the sand, bearing the desert floor beneath you. Flying particles sting your face. You squint to protect your eyes…. And that very reflex is the metaphor God uses to describe His protection for you.

Moses said of God's protection in the wilderness, "He kept him as the apple of his eye" (Deuteronomy 32:10). The "apple of the eye" is the most tender part of the eye. God calling us the apple of His eye signifies His tender love and care for us. It's His assurance that He will protect and care for us through the storm.

However desolate we may *feel,* we are never abandoned by God—not even for a second.

> *Who shall separate us from the love of Christ? shall tribulation, or distress, or persecution, or famine, or nakedness, or peril, or sword? As it is written, For thy sake we are killed all the day long; we are accounted as sheep for the slaughter. Nay, in all these things we are more than conquerors through him that loved us. For I am persuaded, that neither death, nor life, nor angels, nor principalities, nor powers, nor things present, nor things to come, Nor height, nor depth, nor any other*

creature, shall be able to separate us from the love of God,
which is in Christ Jesus our Lord.—ROMANS 8:35–39

It all comes back to resting in God's love and trusting His promises through the storm.

A RIFT IN THE CLOUDS

The hours passed slowly in the hospital for Scott and Nikki and their parents. They took turns trying to keep Lydia distracted, and they grieved for their little girl.

One day, a friend gave Nikki a suggestion by way of a clipped article. The article described a procedure the Hands had never heard of—Live Donor Liver Transplantation (LDLT). In this procedure, the liver donor is living, and he or she only donates a portion of the liver. Because the liver has the capability to regenerate and grow, both the donor and the recipient eventually have a full liver.

Scott and Nikki hopefully shared the information with Lydia's doctor. He nodded in recognition. "Yes, we know about this procedure, but we never suggested it to you because our hospital is not set up to perform the delicate procedure, and none of our surgeons are qualified."

A few days later, Scott and Nikki again approached the doctor. "There just has to be a way to make this work," they pleaded.

The doctor paused and looked hesitantly at Scott and Nikki before he continued. "The university has just hired Dr. Yuri Genyk from New York. He is quite experienced with this procedure. He'll be arriving in Los Angeles within days, and we can ask him if he'll perform the surgeries here."

Scott and Nikki looked at each other in awe. Surely this was no coincidence that the very doctor who could perform the surgery Lydia needed had just been transferred a distance of three thousand miles within days of when it would be too late for Lydia. "Of course, let's do it right away," they said almost simultaneously.

A GIFT OF LOVE

Immediately, the family began the search for the right liver for Lydia. Scott, of course, had the same blood type as his daughter, but his liver was too large. Nikki's blood type was different.

Both of Lydia's grandmothers asked for their blood to be tested, and both were a perfect match. Because Nikki's mom, Sherry, was a few years younger and in perfect health, she was allowed to be the donor.

The surgery couldn't happen soon enough. Lydia's liver was consumed by cirrhosis, and other vital organs were shutting down.

SUNSHINE AFTER THE RAIN

On the morning of the surgeries, Terrie and I drove to the Children's Hospital to wait with the Hand family. Others from our church gathered as well to offer their support. The surgeries would be tricky. Only the Children's Hospital was equipped to perform Lydia's surgery, but they weren't equipped to remove Sherry's liver. Consequently, Sherry's liver had to be hurriedly transported seven miles across Los Angeles between the two hospitals. Additionally, Lydia's surgery was very delicate, and we prayed fervently that the Lord would guide Dr. Genyk's skilled fingers.

Both surgeries went off without a hitch, and one month later, a healthy baby Lydia was released from the hospital.

As Lydia began normal patterns of growth and development, it was apparent that God had used the surgery to bring lasting healing to her tiny body. As of this writing, thirteen years later, Lydia is a healthy and energetic young lady who loves the Lord and brings joy to all who know her. The Lord has also blessed Lydia with a beautiful voice, and she sometimes sings in our church musical presentations. Her bubbly personality and radiant smile are delightful.

THE REST OF THE STORY

The Lord does so much more for us in desert storms than just helping us "make it through." He actually brings good through it—blessings we never would have experienced without the storm.

Eight years after Lydia's transplant, the Lord impressed on Sherry's heart that she should invite all of the doctors in Lydia's transplant team to our church for our annual Friend Day. The transplant coordinator came, and Dr. Genyk came with his twelve-year-old son, Stephen.

My sermon that morning was especially for the many unsaved guests in the service. I carefully and clearly explained God's free offer of salvation through Christ. We were all thrilled when Stephen responded to the invitation after the message and trusted Christ as his Saviour. At lunch that afternoon, the transplant coordinator and Dr. Genyk both confirmed that they were already saved.

"God used Dr. Genyk to save Lydia's life," Sherry beamed, "but He used Lydia's life to save Dr. Genyk's son."

DESERT RAINBOWS

When the dust and rain of a desert storm settle, one can often see a vivid rainbow arched across the sky. Our God has a way of bringing rich beauty after intense storms.

Rainbows, however, are comprised by two unlikely objects—light and water. When ordinary light reflects from a certain angle on ordinary water, it makes an extraordinary display of beauty. Who but God would create such resplendence from objects so common?

Similarly, our God creates rainbows in the lives of ordinary people in desert places. He takes the most unlikely events of our lives and shines the brilliant light of His love upon them to create a bright display of His grace.

Maybe you are an ordinary Christian in a fierce storm. Take hope, friend. You are the apple of God's eye, and He protects you in the shelter of His love. Hold fast to the unchanging promises of God, and, when the wind settles and the rain ceases, you will see the unmistakable grace of God.

I've had the privilege of pastoring many through violent desert storms, and over the years, our family has encountered several of our own. But in every case in which a storm-assaulted Christian has trusted God's goodness and submitted to His leading, I've seen God bring incredible blessings and ministry from the storm—stunning desert rainbows. The most heartening aspect of it all is that these are not super-Christians. They're just ordinary people with an extraordinary God—a God who creates beauty in desert places and rainbows after desert storms.

SEVEN

DESERT TRAINING
WHERE ENDURANCE IS DEVELOPED

"I can tell fatigue when I see it," Bill Lawrence said as he shook my hand after church. We were in the middle of building our main auditorium, and, like most church building programs, it was a stressful and trying time.

"Thanks, Bill," I said, and I relaxed my side of the handshake. But Bill didn't relax. He leaned a little closer. "Listen, why don't you come with me to go hunting on my son's ranch in Oregon? It would give you some time away from this project, and it would give you some much-needed rest."

As thoughtful as the offer was and as much as I enjoy hunting, I declined. For one thing, I didn't feel I had the time. Yes, I was exhausted, but that was because I had a lot to do. And I didn't see time away hunting as being helpful to forward progress! Additionally, I didn't really know Bill well, and I was concerned that the trip would be an imposition on him. I appreciated the offer and left it at that.

A few days later, my secretary handed me an envelope that Bill had dropped by the office that morning. Inside were Southwest Airline tickets to Boise, Idaho. Also enclosed was a hunting license. Determined that I needed a break, Bill had checked my calendar with my secretary and booked a trip to his son's ranch.

Bill's son, Mark, greeted us at the Boise airport when we arrived and helped us load our things into his truck. I learned right away that Mark named all his vehicles, and this one's name was Spec—short for Specimen, a fitting name as I soon learned. Spec had been gifted with generous portions of bailing wire to keep him operable. During much of the three-hour drive from the airport, I wondered if Spec would actually make it to Mark's ranch.

Mark was one of the most unique men I have ever met. He was raised in Lancaster, California, but he had purchased the ranch in eastern Oregon many years prior. He was always happy, easily side-tracked, and ready at any moment to help someone in need. In the days to follow, Mark became a dear friend.

Our first evening of hunting was not entirely successful. I think this was largely due to Mark's eagerness to talk and fellowship along the way, scaring away most of the deer! Later that evening, Mark and I met Bill at the top of a hill in a little ten-by-ten structure that Mark had built as a place to rest when he was hunting in the mountains. Borrowing a name from stories he had read of WWI, Mark called this his "hutment." (He really had a flair for names.)

After we cleared out the mice and rats, we found a place to sit and have some sandwiches. Over the next several hours, I learned much about Mark. This cheerful "man's man" who liked to rough it in the wilderness had a heart for God like few men I've met. Long after our sandwiches were finished, we were still talking about the things of the Lord. Through our conversation, I learned that Mark was in a desert place of decision.

ADVANTAGES OF DESERT TRAINING

Less than 150 miles from Lancaster is Twentynine Palms, California—the United States Marine Corps' largest base. Servicemembers generally dislike this post because of its desolation and isolation. Some even call it by the nickname "29 Stumps."

Yet, the base is valuable to the US military. In addition to the geographic advantages in the desert for air strips, the desert is good for combat training. Here servicemembers can train in similar conditions to the arid Middle Eastern deserts where they may soon find themselves deployed.

Desert training shaped the life of one of the greatest men in the Bible as well. Something about his upbringing in the harsh climate seemed to strengthen his resolve and prepare him for the rigors of ministry. There is no man in Scripture spoken of as favorably as John the Baptist. Jesus said of him, "Among them that are born of women there hath not risen a greater than John the Baptist: notwithstanding he that is least in the kingdom of heaven is greater than he" (Matthew 11:11).

This great man was raised in the desert. Luke 1:80 tells us of his childhood, "And the child grew, and waxed strong in spirit, and was in the deserts till the day of his shewing unto Israel." John learned during his years in the desert how to walk alone with God, which was good, for he would soon stand alone for God.

So if you find yourself in a desert place—a place where it seems too harsh to survive and definitely too isolated to want to linger—take courage. God may be training you for something very special. He may be building in you the courage to stand alone.

A TRIP TO THE DESERT

Where is this desert where you learn to stand alone? It is any place of isolation from the world and intimacy with God.

Sometimes, we find ourselves in the desert by circumstances beyond our control. A single phone call or email can usher you into a loneliness and isolation you would never have chosen. Sometimes we find the desert purposefully by choosing to push away from the distractions surrounding us and asking God for a deeper intimacy with Him.

However you get there, the desert training ground is isolated. The loneliness, and sometimes even spiritual parch, helps us discover the ever near presence of God. It helps us grow in our hunger for Him, and it deepens our desire for *His* approval. It makes us value His presence more than the approval and company of others. It gives us a yearning that will not be quenched except by His fullness in our lives.

All of us can grow soft in our walk with God. We are assaulted with error and surrounded by compromise—on the job, by family, through culture itself. The temptation to yield to the pressure rather than to stand for Christ can seem overwhelming. Sometimes, we need to seek out a desert place to strengthen our resolve and intensify our thirst for our God.

John the Baptist knew the desert well, and he had a spiritual tenacity in his ministry that must have been shaped in its dusty plains. The years he spent on its crusty expanse helped him develop a toughness that refused to yield to the opponent in spiritual battle.

The desert makes us value God's presence more than the approval and company of others.

Sitting in the "hutment" with Bill and Mark Lawrence, I learned that Mark had a desire for this kind of strength. He had been receiving my preaching tapes for some time, and he was coming under conviction about the spiritually lukewarm church he had been attending. He was growing restless, too, concerning the lack of fruit he had been experiencing in his own life.

Several weeks later, Mark, his wife Diane, and their two daughters, Janelle and Brittany, came to Lancaster and visited our church for our Christmas musical. That summer they attended our annual Spiritual Leadership Conference in Lancaster. During this week, Mark's faith and doctrinal position were greatly strengthened, and he knew the Holy Spirit was convicting him to make some changes in his life.

A PLACE OF IDENTIFICATION

At first glance, the desert would seem to be a place of isolation, extreme separation. And, truthfully, it is. In fact, John the Baptist was so separated from the world around him that when he began his ministry, he stood out remarkably from the crowd. Matthew 3:4 describes his appearance: "And the same John had his raiment of camel's hair, and a leathern girdle about his loins; and his meat was locusts and wild honey."

Yet, for John the Baptist, the desert was more a place of *identification* than of *isolation*. Yes, John was separated, but his separation had the purpose of identification with God. Everything about John, from his clothing of camel's hair to his diet of locusts to his message of repentance, boldly proclaimed, "I stand here to represent my God."

Although conformity is comfortable, it is fruitless.

John didn't worry about being in sync with culture. He was far more in touch with God than he was with the world. But John had one of the most fruitful ministries in the Bible. Separation just for the sake of separation misses the mark. But separation for the purpose of identification with Christ is honoring to God.

It's so easy to become conformed to the world in clothing, entertainment, communication, even ministry philosophy. But although conformity is comfortable, it is fruitless. Desert training teaches its students to reject the comfortable and choose the profitable at every point where the two conflict.

SCHOOL OF THE DESERT

Consider for a moment the role of John the Baptist's parents in John's ministry. After all, it was their choice to raise him alone in the deserts of Judea. Surely this was a difficult decision. John's father, Zacharias, was a priest of the Levites of the course of Abiah (Luke 1:5). Josephus tells us there were about twenty thousand priests at that time, but that many of them were corrupt. Somehow Zacharias knew that he needed to protect his son from the influence of those who would turn his heart away from God, so he opted for the desert.

Can you imagine the pressure Zacharias' peers must have placed on him during John's childhood? "Zacharias, where's your son? Why don't you let him spend time with our kids?" "Zacharias, why isn't John in school with our boys? Is he getting an accredited education?" "Zacharias, do you think John is better than our sons? Do you think you're better than us?" Raising John in the desert was a decision requiring great courage on the part of Zacharias and his wife Elisabeth. But it was worth the price. From an early age, John's heart was turned toward the things of the Lord.

Although I don't recommend parents literally take their children to the desert and pitch a tent under a Joshua tree, I do believe they should nurture an environment where their children learn to walk with God. Parents must make choices, sometimes tough choices, to spiritually protect and nurture the hearts of their children. These choices will likely involve their children's friends, education, entertainment, mentors, and many other areas. Wise choices now can greatly affect a child's heart for God and future fruitfulness.

Additionally, wise parents will center their home around God's Word. They will model a consistent walk with God and teach their children to daily read and study His Word. They will ask the Lord to give their children a hunger to know Him. They will involve their children in church and ministry and encourage their children to give godly people (including mom and dad) entrance into their hearts as they mature and make decisions.

This type of "desert training" will create a spiritual thirst in the hearts of young people. As they learn to walk with God, they will have the strength to stand for God when faced with options of compromise.

One of the early changes Mark made for their family was to enroll his daughters, Janelle and Brittany, in our Christian school during the winter months. In addition to school, they also participated in teen activities, and both girls flourished spiritually in this environment.

God used the godly influences in Janelle and Brittany's lives to develop within their hearts spiritual appetites and a godly focus. Both girls chose to come to West Coast Baptist College after graduation.

Yet none of us could have anticipated how important this desert training would soon become.

TRUE COMPASS

Desert training gives perspective to what is really important— walking with God and leading others to Him.

A few weeks after the Spiritual Leadership Conference that Mark attended, I invited him to go with me to make a soulwinning visit. That evening, we had the privilege of visiting a family in Lancaster who needed the Lord in their lives. We were able to see the entire family trust Christ as their Saviour in their home. The mom, the dad, their child, and the grandmother all prayed to receive Christ.

From that moment, Mark's life was entirely changed. He had never seen someone accept Christ in their home, and he was anxious to go out and reach people for the Lord in his hometown of Prairie City, Oregon.

Yes, Mark knew that he was facing some hard decisions regarding separation, but when he saw this kind of spiritual fruit, the choices didn't seem so difficult.

Wise parents will center their home around God's Word.

The drastic change in Mark's life through that one soulwinning visit was beyond what any military sergeant could hope to accomplish in six weeks of basic training. Mark was a changed man, and everyone in Prairie City, Oregon, soon knew it.

Everywhere Mark went he witnessed to anyone who would listen to him. He soon became one of the greatest soulwinners I have ever known. Over the next five years, the Lord allowed Mark, as a lay pastor, to establish a church in Oregon, to win hundreds of people to the Lord, and to become a very effective servant for Jesus. Like John the Baptist, Mark gave his voice to proclaim the truth to others.

VOICE OF TRUTH

John the Baptist's greatest desire was to make the truth known. He identified himself simply as "a voice." John didn't even care if he was liked or appreciated. He didn't even care if people knew or applauded the name behind the voice. He simply knew he had a voice, and he determined to use it for God.

John wasn't a respecter of persons either. He spoke the truth even to Herod when he told the king, "It is not lawful for thee to have thy brother's wife" (Mark 6:18). This ultimately cost John his head. But for a man with the spiritual commitment as John, he would rather lose his life for the truth than live a compromiser.

VOICE OF DECISION

When John committed his voice to the cause of truth, he chose a God-ordained venue of using it—preaching. Twice, Scripture describes John's ministry as a preaching ministry (Matthew 3:1; Luke 3:3).

I remember in the early days of Lancaster Baptist Church standing outside the front door of the church and shaking hands after the service. One man, a visitor, took my hand and said, "Pastor, I can see you have a good heart. But this church is never going to grow the way you are doing it. You need less preaching and more…." I kindly suggested that he find a different church if he wanted less preaching, but I knew that God wanted our church to continue to proclaim the truth.

One of Paul's last instructions to Timothy was, "Preach the word" (2 Timothy 4:2). Preaching is God's method of presenting truth in a way that brings hearers to a point of decision. John didn't simply expend his life serving his community, although I'm sure he was a servant to others. John never performed a miracle, spoke in tongues, or healed anyone. But he preached, and his sermons pointed people to Christ. It was John's preaching that brought people to a point of decision.

Twentieth century missionary, Jim Elliot, was a man who sought out desert-place training. He was killed by the tribal people he was trying to reach with the Gospel, but his journals record the intensity of a man who yearned with his whole heart to know God intimately and be used of Him fully. Like John the Baptist, Jim wanted his voice to be one that led others to decision. On September 19, 1948, he wrote in his journal: "Father, make of me a 'crisis man.' Bring those I contact to decision. Let me not be a milepost on a single road. Make me a fork, so that men must turn one way or another on facing Christ in me."

"Crisis men" are committed to giving others truths they can build their lives upon, which requires they make a decision to embrace those truths. One who has chosen to lend his voice to the support of truth must be willing to be a voice that leads people to decision, even if that decision causes people to turn from him and the truth he speaks.

JOY UNSPEAKABLE

One day, John went as usual out to the Jordan to preach and baptize. As usual, some scorned and mocked. As usual, some responded to his message. Either way, he was faithful to make his voice heard—the voice he had trained in the desert as he learned to walk with God.

But this day, something unusual happened—something which John had spent his entire lifetime anticipating. Jesus appeared.

"John seeth Jesus coming unto him, and saith, Behold the Lamb of God, which taketh away the sin of the world. This is he of whom I said, After me cometh a man which is preferred before me: for he was before me" (John 1:29–30).

Can you imagine the joy John experienced? After thirty years of waiting, training in the desert, speaking as a voice of truth, Jesus appeared. Any rejection John had experienced was trivial in that moment, for his life purpose was fulfilled.

MARK'S LEGACY

It was truly a beautiful June day when Terrie and I arrived at the Lawrence ranch in Oregon for Janelle's wedding. It had been a special delight several months earlier when Janelle met the son of another dear friend, Dr. David Gibbs, Jr., on the campus of West Coast Baptist College. Soon love was in the air, and I was invited to perform the wedding ceremony for Janelle and J.D. on the family ranch.

Many friends had gathered in the rolling pasture, where a beautiful gazebo had been set up for the ceremony. Ribboned chairs surrounded the gazebo, and were already filling up. In the background, the Strawberry Mountains had patches of snow on their peaks. All of us were thrilled to see God bringing these two choice young people together to serve Him.

Just a few days after the wedding, Mark took his younger daughter, Brittany, on a flight in their private plane. They swooped over the Strawberry Mountains and surveyed the ranch from the air. After their flight, Mark and Brittany took a ride on their four-wheeler. Tragically, just as they were ending their ride, Mark fell off, and his head struck a boulder. He was rushed to the hospital where he spent nine days in the Critical Care Unit. On July 5, 2006, the Lord took him home.

More than a thousand people gathered in the auditorium of Lancaster Baptist Church for Mark's memorial service. Many testified of how Mark had touched their lives, and many shared how he had led them to Christ. A few days later, hundreds of friends and pastors from the Northwest gathered at the Lawrence ranch for the Mark's funeral service. The grace of God was extremely evident, and several accepted Christ as their Saviour.

DESERT TRAINING FOR ETERNAL GLORY

When I think back to the night with Mark in the hutment, the evening with him out soulwinning, and the decisions he made soon after to live and stand without compromise, I'm very thankful. I can't imagine the joy with which he stood before the Lord when he was unexpectedly ushered into glory.

The hunting trips I shared with Mark Lawrence will always be special memories in my heart. Truly they were times of refreshment and re-energizing for the ministry. But those things are temporal.

More important is the fruit Mark's life still bears today, and it all goes back to his desert training. Right here, in the Mojave Desert, God transformed Mark's life. He was a rancher and hunter who became a soulwinner, pastor, and vibrant servant of God. Even now, as I am out and about in the community, I meet people who tell me they met Mark—he shared a Gospel tract with them, or he led them to the Lord.

And Mark's fruitfulness continues through his family. Diane remains faithful to the Lord and a dear friend of our family. The Lord has used the desert training Mark and Diane gave their daughters to give them the strength they needed even when they lost their dad. Both Janelle and Brittany are serving the Lord today, a legacy to Mark's dedication to God.

Mark's life is a prod to me to choose the hard path where necessary and to be faithful even in the desert places of training.

When you find yourself in the desert, remember that these places are times of preparation and enabling for future ministry. What is God calling you to do? What decisions is He prompting you to make? What truth is He asking you to proclaim?

Our most natural tendency is to resist the desert isolation and reject the training. But when we, like John the Baptist—and Mark Lawrence, embrace the desert and allow God to transform us through it, we will have ministry that bears eternal fruit.

DESERT DESIRE
HOW CHRIST IS EXALTED

E arly in my ministry, the Lord birthed a vision in my heart to develop Christian leaders through establishing a Bible college on the West Coast. In the fall of 1995, that vision became a reality when our church opened the doors of West Coast Baptist College.

So many people sacrificed in those first years. Our church family believed in the purpose and philosophy of the college and actively supported it through giving, serving, and laboring above and beyond the call of duty.

Our early staff and faculty gave of themselves without reservations to train the forty-three students we had that first year. They worked diligently, and sometimes creatively, to use our limited facilities to provide a quality education for these future servants of God.

The students themselves demonstrated exceptional hearts for God as they slept and lived in improvised housing arrangements the first few years and attended class in modular buildings.

We were all thankful for what God had done—and what we knew He was going to do—through this college that He was raising up. It was our desire to see our students graduate and bear much fruit for the glory of God.

Our first construction projects for the college were dormitories, made possible by the generous and sacrificial gifts of our church family and pastors and churches around the country who believed in what we were trying to accomplish. Next to housing accommodations, our greatest facility need was an educational building with adequate classroom space and equipment. As the college grew, this need became more obvious, and we prayed fervently for the Lord to help us build such a building. When God answered our prayers, He did so in an intricate and surprising series of events.

DESERT DESIRES

The desert has a way of economizing extravagant wish lists. A trek through its hot wastelands usually leaves travelers longing for something other than fancy GPS units or sophisticated binoculars. The empty-handed hiker in the desert will soon find his desires streamlined to the most basic of necessities.

This cutting away is one of the benefits God works in our hearts in desert places. We're born natural gluttons for recognition and attention. But God sometimes leads us to desert places that He might refine our desires to the central purpose of life—that *He* would be glorified.

When John the Baptist left the desert of Judea to begin his public ministry, he had one desire. It wasn't to gain a large following or nationwide recognition. It wasn't to be known and appreciated. It was simply to point as many people as possible to Christ.

As John began his ministry, he did, in fact, gain a large following, and he did gain the recognition of his nation. But when Jesus appeared on the scene, John's disciples became troubled at a noticeable shift in John's popularity: "And they came unto John, and said unto him, Rabbi, he that was with thee beyond Jordan, to whom thou barest witness, behold, the same baptizeth, and all men come to him" (John 3:26).

John's response to his waning popularity stands in bold relief to the pride of his disciples. "He must increase," John replied, "but I must decrease" (John 3:30). This is the desire of a man whom God will use.

AN EXPENSIVE DESIRE

Ask any Christian, "Do you want Christ to be glorified?" and the answer will, of course, be "Yes!" But consider what this answer cost John the Baptist. Christ *in*creasing meant that John's influence and ministry was *de*creasing!

It's easy to *say* we want Christ to be exalted, but are we willing for His exaltation to come at our expense? We naturally rebel at losing anything we hold dear—including our pride, but death to self is the only way we can truly exalt Christ.

When John's disciples complained about Jesus' popularity, they missed the entire purpose of John's ministry—pointing people to the Messiah. So when John decreased in popularity, he actually increased in fulfilling his purpose.

Most Christians look only at the *expense* of death to self, but in doing so, they forget the *benefit*. We were not created to satisfy or promote ourselves, and we can never be happy doing so. We were created to honor the Lord. Although maintaining a desire like John the Baptist's may seem costly, we are the true beneficiaries.

If the increasing of Jesus was a divine necessity for John the Baptist, how much more so for us! Our goal should be that Christ's work would go forward and His name be exalted.

WHERE HUMILITY FLOURISHES

Not much can survive in the desert, including pride. When a man or woman learns to truly walk with God in desert places, one byproduct is genuine humility. Since humility doesn't require the constant approval or praise of man, it can flourish in the lonely plains, basking and growing in the smile of God alone.

When John the Baptist began his ministry, the priests asked him, "Who art thou? that we may give an answer to them that sent us. What sayest thou of thyself?" (John 1:22). They wanted to place a label on him to properly categorize him for their ecclesiastical museum. This would have been John's chance to explain his valuable purpose. He could have said, "I'm the man who Malachi prophesied of four hundred years ago. I'm important. Watch my ministry!"

Yet John didn't try to impress them with a title, his credentials, or his lineage. He didn't proclaim himself as the great forerunner of the Messiah, although he was. Rather, he simply said of himself, "I am the voice of one crying in the wilderness, Make straight the way of the Lord" (John 1:23). To John, the message he had to give was far more important than a title or an accolade.

Pride always undermines the work of God.

Pride always undermines the work of God in the home, in relationships, in the church, and among other believers. Yet maintaining a humble spirit is the great challenge of every Christian's life and of every ministry.

DEATH IN THE DESERT

Each spring, Lancaster celebrates the bloom of our state flower with a California Poppy Festival. Areas of the desert are clothed in radiant blankets of wild poppies.

The California poppy has a remarkably short lifespan. Like other desert annuals, it blooms profusely for a few weeks and then dies, leaving its hardy seeds in the desert soil. Those lonely seeds wait for the next spring rains and then burst with life and color. The death the desert heat brings to the poppy plant actually provides for new life the next spring.

The desert places of our lives also provide opportunity for self to die. We want desperately to preserve our pride, to protect our reputation, to preserve our image; but only by dying to self can the life of Christ be seen in us.

One of the greatest opportunities to die to self is when criticism, slander, or persecution push us out of the favor of others into a desert place. Our natural tendency is to build a quick road of escape out of the desert—to defend our rights and reclaim our pride. But, when we do so, we usually miss seeing God's glory in that very desert place.

STRATEGIC LANDSCAPING

Early in my ministry at Lancaster, I made a decision that I believe has helped the work of the Lord to flourish in our desert. I determined that our ministry would not be entangled in divisive concerns that centered on personalities, but rather that we would focus on winning souls here and nurturing hearts for God.

There are many doctrinal concerns that I believe should never be compromised. For these, we've stood and willingly borne the criticism that accompanies such stands. Yet, among those who believe the same doctrine we hold dear, there is sometimes another variety of strife perpetrated, much of which is rooted in pride. These issues often are most prevalent in "preacher circles" and relate to camps or associations or fellowships. Although I've committed to never compromise truth, I never want the young Christians at our church stumbling over the pride of Christian leaders in other ministries, thus I've refrained from being involved in these types of arguments.

There simply is not enough water in the desert to feed weeds *and* grow flowers. I wanted our church to be focused on planting the seed of the Gospel and then growing hearts for God. Anything that would threaten this growth must be avoided.

OPPORTUNITY TO DIE TO SELF

It can be difficult to focus on watering the grass when others are intent on transplanting weeds into your yard! Like anyone attempting to do a work for God, I faced my share of weed-planters. As God blessed Lancaster Baptist Church, some tried to sideline or ostracize us. Others tried to discredit, and still others pushed us to choose personality-based loyalties. But we were involved in intense labor—growing hearts for God in the desert, and we couldn't afford to shift our focus. When we avoided these pride-centered issues, some began slinging mud.

On one occasion, during a time of particular blessing and growth in our church, I received a newsletter from a church on the East Coast. This newsletter had been mailed to several thousand pastors across America. It lacked a Christ-centered philosophy, and its tone was caustic. The editors had constructed a rambling analysis of various Baptist churches. My name and the names of several other pastors were labeled with the word "compromise" because we did not espouse the exact methods or employ the same special speakers as the editors' churches.

Of course there was an initial desire to defend the integrity of our ministry by responding to the pastor who sent the newsletter. I thank God, however, for a few praying friends whose help caused me to keep those really insignificant issues in perspective and keep on with the main work of winning souls for Christ.

As we continued to exalt Christ's name and give for His work to go forward, He blessed our ministry. Our facilities seemed smaller and smaller as more people were reached, and the needs for better college facilities became glaringly apparent.

DIVINE RELATIONSHIPS

One of the friends who helped me maintain perspective during that difficult season was Dr. Don Sisk. Dr. Sisk has a contagious joy and enthusiasm that has blessed me ever since I met him, and I treasure his godly mentoring and friendship in my life.

A veteran missionary to Japan, Dr. Sisk was for many years the General Director of BIMI. About the time our ministry was openly criticized, Dr. Sisk met another man who God would use greatly in our ministry in the future—Dr. Clayton Revels.

Soon after their meeting, Dr. Revels experienced a similar criticism to that which we had experienced, and his came from some of the same people. The Lord used the Sisks to minister to the Revels during this time, and their hearts were knit in close friendship.

In 2003, Dr. Sisk prepared to retire from his position as General Director at BIMI. When he told me of this change, I couldn't help but think of the investment he could make into the lives of young people if he would come to West Coast Baptist College and serve as our chairman of the missions program. He graciously agreed, and soon he and his wife, Virginia, were here teaching one full semester each year.

When the Revels decided to retire a few months later, they expressed to the Sisks that they would like to contribute some money to West Coast Baptist College.

When Dr. Sisk first met the Revels, he had no knowledge of their personal finances, but, over the years, as the Revels made significant offerings to missions through BIMI, their generous hearts revealed their financial prosperity. Now the Sisks were excited to have a part in helping the Revels help our college.

Dr. Revels and his wife, Mildred, planned to visit that spring so they could see the college. Tragically, Mildred was diagnosed with a fast-growing brain tumor before they could make the trip. Weeks later, she entered the presence of the Lord.

At Mildred's funeral, Dr. Revels reiterated again to Dr. Sisk that he wanted to visit the college, and, in honor of his wife's burden for the school, he wanted to help us financially. He planned a trip for October, during our annual missions conference.

DESERT DELIGHT

The result of death in the desert is new life. Just as the seed from the dead poppies yields new poppies, so the Gospel seed planted by Christians who have crucified self yields fruit that abounds to the glory of God. Jesus instructed His disciples, "Except a corn of wheat fall into the ground and die, it abideth alone: but if it die, it bringeth forth much fruit" (John 12:24).

John the Baptist's ability to decrease for Christ's increase was rooted in his delight for leading others to Christ. Like a groomsman who knows the true focus of the wedding is on the bride and groom, John rejoiced in Christ's appearance rather than personal recognition. He specifically directed his followers to the salvation only Christ could offer when he explained, "He that believeth on the Son hath everlasting life: and he that believeth not the Son shall not see life; but the wrath of God abideth on him" (John 3:36). John's delight was in souls coming to Christ.

If our desire is for Christ to increase, our delight will be to see others trust in Him for salvation. Jesus specifically told us that He is glorified by the spiritual fruit that we bear: "Herein is my Father glorified, that ye bear much fruit…" (John 15:8).

If our desire is for Christ to increase, our delight will be to see others trust in Him for salvation.

When Dr. Revels visited Lancaster Baptist Church and West Coast Baptist College, he immediately related to the soulwinning efforts and emphasis on missions that he saw here. He fell in love with the school, the students, and what we were working to accomplish. He wanted to invest in the future laborers for harvest, and made several large financial gifts which helped us begin construction on a three-story, beautiful educational building. We named the building in his honor, and it is currently used seven days a week in the Lord's work.

The Revels Building stands today as a monument to God's glory. God used the divine encounter of two men whose greatest desire is to bring Him glory to help build this building. When Dr. Revels was maligned, he remained faithful to the Lord and refused to become bitter. Through that, the Lord orchestrated his friendship with Dr. Sisk, and the Revels were blessed by the Sisk's ministry of encouragement. Ultimately, our college has been greatly blessed by both of these men.

But that's really not the end of the story. The publication of the slanderous newsletter years earlier, my friendship with Dr. Sisk, Dr. Sisk's friendship with Dr. Revels, and the gift of Dr. Revels for the educational building all culminated in an amazing afternoon meeting.

WHERE CHRIST IS EXALTED

Several months after the Revels Building was completed, the pastor who had previously published the newsletter that labeled me as a compromiser and had so deeply hurt Dr. Revels made a special trip to California to visit. The Lord had given me the opportunity to help his son, and, through that kindness, the Holy Spirit convicted this pastor of his earlier criticism. Now he came to Lancaster to apologize in person.

I was deeply thankful that he would make this trip and that he desired mutual fellowship. We had a sweet time of restoration and prayer in my office. We embraced, and I silently thanked the Lord for His grace in the desert. Through the desire of many to exalt Christ, remain faithful in service, and promote His work, God was glorified.

DESIRE, DEATH, AND DELIGHT

Only God could order a plan that requires an unlikely means—death—to bring a miraculous result—life.

The desire of a man who longs for Christ to be exalted is only realized by death—his own. When he has died to self and invests his labor in the increase of Christ, his greatest delight becomes what God has ordained to be the fruit of his death—souls saved to the glory of God.

Is exalting Christ your greatest desire? Is it a strong enough desire that you are willing to die for it? What about to live for it while dying to self?

All of us are quick to protect our names and further our agendas. But when God leads us to desert places where self is diminished, He makes it obvious that the only life worth living is that laid down for the kingdom of God. And He transforms our desires so that our greatest delight is living by God's grace for His glory.

NINE

DESERT REVIVAL
WHY COMPROMISE IS NOT AN OPTION

When Alis Odenthal first saw our church ads broadcasted on Channel 3, the local television station where she worked, she had no idea of the journey of healing and restoration she was about to begin. But she did know that she needed help. Several months earlier, she and her husband, Richard, had separated, leaving both with deep wounds and torn hearts.

Alis' first visit to Lancaster Baptist was during our annual winter revival meeting with Evangelist John Goetsch. His sermon resonated in her soul, and she visited again the next Sunday, and again the next, and the next. Several weeks later, Alis trusted Christ as her Saviour and made her decision public in baptism.

In addition to working for Channel 3, Alis did some freelance work as a musician. One of her jobs was to sing for another church in town. On Sundays, she would come to our early service (we had two identical services each Sunday morning to make room for everyone) and then go to the other church for work. When the other church changed service times, Alis was no longer able to come to our morning service. Not being in the habit of attending our Sunday evening or midweek services, she dropped out of church all together. The following year, Alis and Richard divorced.

From both a spiritual and relational standpoint, the hopeful rays of Alis' life seemed to be dimmed. But God wasn't finished yet.

DESERT SOLITUDE

For all the undesirability of the desert, it does have a distinct advantage—solitude. The world doesn't exactly beat a path out to the middle of nowhere. Thus the desert's seclusion makes it a sanctuary for those willing to seek it.

The chief advantage of this dusty sanctuary is its ability to provide a refuge from the incessant noises calling for our attention and allow us to focus on God. We're bombarded with noise—electronic, social, relational. From every angle, something is demanding a piece of our lives. For many, the very constancy of noise has dulled their hearing so they no longer notice it. But its effect is no less real in their lives.

Much of the noise is produced by a godless culture and transmitted to us through every angle possible—television, news, coworkers, social media, advertisements, etc.; it simply inundates our lives. The danger is that our continual exposure to this noise can desensitize our spirits to the still small voice of God.

But a trip to the desert can fix this problem.

CALL TO THE DESERT

Let's revisit the Israelites in Egypt. The culture in which they lived exposed them to pagan idolatry and drew their attention away from their true God. So God called His people out of Egypt and into the desert where they could worship Him: "And afterward Moses and Aaron went in, and told Pharaoh, Thus saith the LORD God of Israel, Let my people go, that they may hold a feast unto me in the wilderness" (Exodus 5:1).

Throughout the Bible God has called His people out of the pollution of the world and to Himself. The very word *church* used in the New Testament is from the Greek word *ecclesia*, which means "called out." God has designed the church to be a place where we can pull aside from both the filth and distractions of the world and focus on Him.

In 2 Corinthians 6:17–18, God pleads with His people, "Wherefore come out from among them, and be ye separate, saith the Lord, and touch not the unclean thing; and I will receive you, And will be a Father unto you, and ye shall be my sons and daughters, saith the Lord Almighty." The choice to separate from the world leads us to desert worship and gives us an extra measure of closeness with our heavenly Father.

REVIVAL

Since January 1987, we have encouraged our people to seek desert solitude and revival by having an annual series of winter revival meetings. Each year we've had the same preacher—Dr. John Goetsch. And every year God has used this time in a mighty way in our church.

Our church family takes these meetings seriously. We often fast together for a month before the meetings, eliminating different types of "noise" from our lives to ask the Lord to meet with us. Months in advance, our members mark these dates on their calendars and do all they can to be at each evening service. Even the services themselves have much of the announcements and singing streamlined to allow for a longer time of preaching. We want God to speak to our hearts—to revive our relationship with Him and our service for Him.

God has blessed these meetings in special ways over the years, helping us to renew our hearts for Him. For many, the revival also revitalizes their personal worship, helping them to create or refresh their own daily desert solitudes with the Lord.

THE JOURNEY THAT WILL CHANGE YOUR LIFE

In our fast-paced culture, we feel we're doing well to focus on the Lord for a five minute period once a day, or maybe one hour on Sundays. But God called His people out for a *three day journey*. He wanted so much more than a passing piece of attention. He wanted them to commit to a *journey* of long-term, life-changing worship.

Desert worship is multifaceted. It begins with a heart that has personally communed with God both through private quiet time with the Lord and corporate worship in church. But desert worship doesn't end with personal communion. It affects our very lifestyle.

Average Christianity suggests that giving God one hour on Sundays is plenty. Then the rest of the week, the Christian is free to live for selfish pursuits. This isn't what God had in mind when He called His people to worship Him in the desert. He actually wants to change our lives.

Numerous times, Scripture tells us that our God is a jealous God (Exodus 20:5, 34:14; Deuteronomy 4:24). He wants our worship completely given to Him at all times. Just as a husband cannot claim that he loves his wife *and* several other women, so we cannot love God purely while at the same time giving our loyalty and love to conflicting pursuits. Our worship of God must include every area of our lives. We must joyfully submit our wills to His direction.

Committing to desert worship sets us on a pathway of blessing. It is a journey that will change our lives. This is what God did for Alis Odenthal, and then for Richard through her.

BACK ON THE TRAIL

About ten years after Alis stopped attending Lancaster Baptist Church, she found herself once again on our campus when she was asked to sing at a funeral for my dear friend and state senator Pete Knight, which was conducted at our church. As she drove into the parking lot for a rehearsal the afternoon before the funeral, she felt embarrassed and nervous since she had been out of church for so long. She wondered if anyone would recognize her and, if they did, how they would feel about seeing her there to sing.

Just as she got out of her car, my secretary, Bonnie Ferrso, was leaving work for the day, and they met in the parking lot. "Alis! Is that you?" she called as she hurried over to give Alis a hug. "I've been praying for you for ten years!" This chance remark impacted Alis deeply and freed her emotionally to return to Lancaster Baptist.

The next Sunday, Alis was back in church, and several ladies reached out to her. A Sunday school teacher of one of our ladies' classes took her to lunch and invited her to class. Sherry Marquez befriended her. My wife, Terrie, went by the house to visit. The combined efforts of these and others assured Alis that our church loved her and wanted to help her grow in the Lord. Soon, she was back in church, flourishing spiritually, and helping in both Sunday school and the church choir.

SURPRISE TURNS

Alis was sorting and moving storage in her home one day a couple of years later when she came across some pictures and a few other items that she thought Richard would like to have. Although the two had not spoken to each other for twelve years, she searched for his last place of work online. She mailed the pictures and wondered if they would find their way to him.

Unbeknownst to Alis, God was already working in Richard's heart in a unique way. Since the couple's separation in 1993, Richard had continued in his consulting career, with remarkable success. But in 2004, he realized that nothing in his life was truly satisfying. When he found himself on the floor of his den crying and asking the Lord for guidance, he decided to return to the church of his youth, the Catholic church.

Richard began attending church regularly, but, in his words, "Something was missing. I had no personal relationship with the Lord and no guarantee of salvation." The Holy Spirit was bringing a deep unrest and spiritual dissatisfaction in Richard's soul.

At the same time, the Holy Spirit began convicting Richard regarding his relationship with Alis. Two months after Alis sent the pictures to Richard, he called her. The two met for dinner a few days after Thanksgiving 2006.

NEW DIRECTIONS

At the restaurant, Alis told Richard that she had been saved and was now very involved in our church. Richard was alarmed. From his Catholic paradigm, "being saved" was exactly what he did not want. He explained to her that he was now attending mass and active in the Catholic church. Unless she changed her mind about being "born again," Richard thought that was one point on which they would never agree.

They continued meeting and talking, however, and Richard noticed there had been a change in Alis since her salvation. He was still uncomfortable about his relationship with God. Even though he was involved in his church, he knew there was a disconnect somewhere. About a month after he and Alis had their first meeting, he asked her if he could visit one of our services with her.

Richard attended our church on the first Sunday of 2007. As he entered the church, he saw the look of shock on the faces of two men who had previously worked for him in the sheriff's department. (Richard was a retired captain for the Los Angeles County Sheriff's Department, and he had served as commander at the West Hollywood Station.) Richard just wasn't the type of guy who they anticipated coming to church, especially a Baptist church.

"As I sat listening to Pastor Chappell," Richard said later, "I had two thoughts: Pastor knew I was sitting there (because he was preaching about stuff that concerned me), and I had found what had been missing from my life with the Lord."

Richard began attending our church regularly. First he made an early trip to mass (as an extra precaution), and then he joined Alis for our morning service. Several weeks and much follow up later, Richard put his complete faith in Christ as his Saviour.

JOURNEYING TOGETHER

Richard and Alis were both growing rapidly in their relationship with the Lord and in Christian living. In the process of that growth, the Lord turned their hearts toward one another. Richard said, "Once I was saved, the real hard work began for us.

We prayed, read our Bibles (together and individually), sought counseling, and talked for hour upon hour."

It was precious to see this couple fall in love with each other. And it was a joy to see them reunited in marriage in late October 2008. God had taken a once shared, but later divided journey and re-merged their paths.

Now Alis and Richard were committed to experiencing desert revival—together.   They wanted to build their newly established home on God's principles and in God's service.

THE PULL TO STAY OUT OF THE DESERT

It's a predictable phenomenon. Just as soon as someone determines to experience desert revival, Satan attempts to block the way. We may wonder what God could do in desert places, but Satan knows the potential, and he does everything in his power to keep us *out* of the desert.

When Moses stood before Pharaoh and related God's command, "Let my people go!" Pharaoh flatly refused. "And Pharaoh said, Who is the LORD, that I should obey his voice to let Israel go? I know not the LORD, neither will I let Israel go" (Exodus 5:2). He had other plans for the Israelites—to continue making his bricks! Pharaoh wasn't about to let them go.

God answered Pharaoh's question, "Who is the LORD?" with the incredible plagues of Egypt. Pharaoh soon realized that he had made a mistake in denying Moses' request, but he still wasn't about to lose the slave labor of the Israelites. He proposed a series of three compromises to keep the Israelites from the desert journey to which God had called them. All three of these are similar to the compromises Satan presents us with today.

NOT TOO FAR

Pharaoh's first compromise was a demand for proximity—you can sacrifice; just don't leave Egypt. "And Pharaoh called for Moses and for Aaron, and said, Go ye, sacrifice to your God *in the land*" (Exodus 8:25, emphasis added).

Moses protested, so Pharaoh partially relented. They could leave, he said, but not too far. "And Pharaoh said, I will let you go, that ye may sacrifice to the LORD your God in the wilderness; *only ye shall not go very far away...*" (Exodus 8:28, emphasis added).

This is a favorite temptation of the devil, especially for young people. "You can love God," he suggests, "but don't go too far with it. You don't want to look radical!"

There are *unsaved* people who are willing to include God in their lives if it isn't difficult or too altering of their lifestyles. But this is not the journey to which God calls His people. He wants us to give Him everything.

Desert revival doesn't take place in Egypt, and if we want it, we must replace the slogan "don't go too far," with a solid commitment to go all the way. We must completely submit to God's leading and to whole-heartedly embrace His ways.

DON'T TAKE OTHERS

Pharaoh's next offer to Moses was that the men could go, but they should leave their wives and children behind (Exodus 10:11).

The devil is an expert at dividing families, and he often does so by enticing part of the family to lag behind spiritually.

When God brought our family to Lancaster, I had a deep conviction that I wanted to pastor a church that developed strong families and trained men to be the spiritual leader in their homes. I'm thankful for the many godly men in our church who have indeed chosen this role—through personally pursuing a close relationship with Christ and then leading their families in the ways of the Lord. They pray with their wives, and they encourage their hearts in the things of the Lord. They lead their family in daily devotions, and they seek to nurture their children's relationship with the Lord.

One of the special delights in seeing the Odenthals remarry has been watching them grow in the Lord together—as a family. The synergy effect of a joint decision to experience desert revival aids both individuals on the journey.

LEAVE A DEPOSIT

When Moses insisted on a three-day journey with all of the Israelites, Pharaoh proposed one last compromise: don't take your things: "And Pharaoh called unto Moses, and said, Go ye, serve the LORD; only let your flocks and your herds be stayed…" (Exodus 10:24). Pharaoh knew the Israelites' hearts would be tied to their finances, which in their case, was livestock. Basically, he was suggesting their flocks and herds be left as a deposit, insuring their return to Egypt.

Moses would have nothing to do with this compromise, however. "And Moses said, Thou must give us also sacrifices and burnt offerings, that we may sacrifice unto the LORD our God. Our cattle also shall go with us; there shall not an hoof be left behind; for thereof must we take to serve the LORD our God; and we know not with what we must serve the LORD, until we come thither" (Exodus 10:25–26). Moses knew that worship includes sacrifice.

God doesn't command us to give to meet His needs. God's plan of giving is for our benefit.

Satan today still tries to suggest that we can worship the Lord without giving. People who buy into this compromise miss the whole point of giving. God doesn't command us to give to meet *His* needs. He could easily have designed for His work to go forward without tithes and offerings. God's plan of giving is for *our* benefit.

Less than a year and a half after the Odenthals were remarried, Richard gave a testimony in church about his salvation and its impact on his giving:

Many people would believe that all that has taken place so far would be enough, but salvation changes people forever. For me, salvation presented a whole new opportunity to give to the Lord. A fundamental change for me has been in the concept of giving. Before I was saved I lived on the world's economy for sixty years. Salvation required a significant change in my economic management. I didn't get a federal bailout but I did get a Heaven sent bailout. As I began to give here, first with the tithe, then other giving programs, the Lord made sure I was able to meet my commitments. We tithe, contribute to the building program, and missions and other projects as often as we can.

The act of giving can be an act of worship, and it helps us ascribe in our own hearts the glory due to the Lord. This is why Jesus said, "For where your treasure is, there will your heart be also" (Matthew 6:21).

If Satan can convince us to yield on any one of these three compromises—commitment, family, or giving—he can substantially minimize the effect of our desert journey. And our decision to yield to his deception will withhold us from desert revival.

WHAT TO EXPECT IN THE DESERT

Would you like to find this desert place of revival? There's good news for you. Desert revival is accessible to anyone who embraces the solitude of communion with God and is willing to maintain a heart and life separated unto Him.

Christ still calls His disciples to solitude. In Luke 9:10, Scripture records, "And he took them, and went aside privately into a desert place belonging to the city called Bethsaida." He wants us to give Him our complete love and attention—to worship Him with our hearts and our actions.

Yes, a trip to the desert may appear foreboding. (Most people don't choose to live in the desert for the sheer pleasure of the landscape!) Yet, for the heart set on God, a journey to the desert's solitude is an adventure of revival.

TEN

DESERT SUNSETS
WHEN DISCOURAGEMENT SETS IN

January 1, 1989 found the Migliore family making good on their new year's resolution to get into a church. I first saw Dan and Pennie and their two children sitting about halfway back in the auditorium, and I noticed their careful attention to the message. What I didn't know was what had prompted the family to decide church was a necessity.

Several years earlier, Dan and Pennie had adopted their daughter, Angie. Angie was a delightful child, but she was also a difficult child in many ways. As she reached her teen years, the difficulties intensified, and Dan and Pennie knew they needed help.

Two Sundays later, the family walked the aisle during the invitation and trusted Christ. They asked to be baptized immediately, and they quickly began to grow.

Dan's growth was particularly memorable to me because he would stop by my office almost daily on his return commute from work. He'd have a notebook and several questions he had jotted down as they came to his mind throughout the day. Most of them started with "why" or "what." "Pastor, why did my Catholic Bible have extra books?" "What does the Bible say about giving?" "Why do we observe the Lord's Table as often as we do?" "What should I do next to grow?" These were basic questions, but I loved them. And asking them brought solid growth to Dan's life.

Before long, Dan and Pennie were working as record keepers in the youth ministry. Their meticulous attention to detail was a tremendous blessing to our youth pastor. They were active soulwinners and supportive church members. The energy of their love for their church was encouraging and contagious.

Angie got plugged in to the youth group and, through much counseling and encouragement, she began doing better. Outgoing, with a spunky, engaging personality, Angie became one of the best teenage soulwinners I have known. She had a tremendous burden for the lost, and still today, twenty years later, we have a family in our church that Angie led to the Lord.

But even as she grew, Angie continued to struggle. One night, the police arrived on the Migliore's doorstep at 2:00 AM with heartwrenching, tragic news that changed their lives forever. Angie had been murdered.

Dan called me, and a few minutes later, I stood with the Migliore family in their living room. There, in the middle of the night, we wept and prayed and talked about the night season this family would now endure.

NIGHTS IN THE DESERT

Over the years, I've had the sober privilege of weeping with many families in our church through their night seasons. One of the deepest sources of comfort during these times is the Psalms. Many psalms utter low groans of agony and raw expressions of emotion. Yet, they also record words of praise as the psalmist catches a fresh glimpse of the mercy and grace of a faithful God.

Psalm 102, in particular, was penned by a man who was no stranger to grief. Though the identity of the human author is not readily apparent, I believe it was David. As he wrote this Psalm, he was carrying a weighty burden and felt a lonely hopelessness setting in. His metaphors of desert life reveal the desolation he knew. Yet, even as he poured out his burden to the Lord, he experienced the grace of almighty God—grace greater than the darkest night.

A FERVENT PLEA

Without introduction or words of explanation, Psalm 102 opens with a direct cry for help, "Hear my prayer, O LORD, and let my cry come unto thee" (Psalm 102:1). This is the plea of a desperate man baring his soul to the Lord. He is beyond ritualistic routines or melodramatic shows in prayer. He needs God's intervention.

Sometimes our prayers are mere words of repetition, but when we come to an overwhelming time of desperation and we need strength, help, deliverance, and comfort, our prayers become earnest. Sunsets have a way of bringing into our prayers the urgency we should experience every day.

A FEARFUL PRAYER

Like children left alone in the dark, we're prone to feel that God has forsaken us during night seasons of life. The psalmist expressed this fear when he continued his prayer, "Hide not thy face from me in the day when I am in trouble; incline thine ear unto me: in the day when I call answer me speedily" (Psalm 102:2).

As the usual light sources in our lives fade, we may lose our perception of God's nearness and be held in fear's cruel grasp. But just because we can't see God's face, doesn't mean He is absent. God never forsakes His own.

OVERKILL?

If you've never experienced a night alone in the desert, you might read a Psalm like this and wonder, "Why is he being such a crybaby? Why doesn't he just go to the men's prayer meeting, make a request, and move on?" The tears, the hopelessness, the desperation are easily misperceived as hyped sensationalism or dismissed as exaggerated emotionalism by someone who has never been there.

But as we read through this Psalm, we understand more of the reason for the tears and fears. The psalmist voiced three areas of diminishing light in his life.

SUNSETS OF HEALTH

For my days are consumed like smoke, and my bones are burned as an hearth....My days are like a

shadow that declineth; and I am withered like grass.
—Psalm 102:3, 11

Failing health is a poignant reminder of the brevity of life. Even as wood is consumed into fading smoke, so our lives are eventually expended. This realization is painful for a person who still wants to invest more years into others.

Not only did the psalmist realize his days were depleted, but in the process, his body was declining. He described his weakness in verse 3, "...my bones are burned as an hearth." The bones are the strongest part of the body, but his seemed to be merely charcoal dust in the fireplace.

So many dear members of our church have gone through sunsets of health, and I have often been humbled and blessed by the grace I've seen in their lives as they've clung to the Lord's faithfulness through these difficult seasons.

Even in our own family, we've walked through nights that we weren't sure how they would end. In October of 2009, our son, Larry, was diagnosed with a fast-growing cancer that required immediate surgery followed by intense chemotherapy. Through Larry's surgeries, treatment, and healing, I learned in a more personal way than ever before of the intensity of sunsets of health. Yet, God's grace was so manifest in Larry's life during this trial, that we all have grown closer to the Lord through it.

We can (and should) do our best to care for our bodies and avail ourselves of available remedies, but ultimately, only God can prescribe our health. With the advanced medical care that we enjoy in America, we subconsciously believe that there *must* be a cure for anything—if we go to the right doctor, he'll somehow fix it. But when we come to a point where there is no pill we can take or procedure we can follow to make us better, we realize how helpless and feeble we truly are. Life, death, and even health are in the hands of the Lord.

SUNSETS OF THE HEART

My heart is smitten, and withered like grass; so that I forget to eat my bread. By reason of the voice of my groaning my bones cleave to my skin.—PSALM 102:4–5

Like the fatigue at the end of a long day, desert sunsets can bring an overwhelming sense of emotional exhaustion. In Psalm 102, David related this exhaustion to grass withered in the desert heat. He wanted to stand strong and rejoice, but he couldn't.

David's trials were so mentally and emotionally consuming that he forgot to eat. The pain of his soul literally affected his body. He was completely depleted.

I don't know how many times I've stood in a hospital waiting room with a dear church member as they've experienced grief so wrenching it took their appetite. I'd offer to pick up lunch for them. "No thank you, I can't eat," they'd respond. I, too, have experienced this agony, and I know the insufficiency of human props to support a withered heart. Only God's grace can provide the replenishment needed.

SUNSETS OF HOPE

I am like a pelican of the wilderness: I am like an owl of the desert. I watch, and am as a sparrow alone upon

the house top. Mine enemies reproach me all the day;
and they that are mad against me are sworn against
me. For I have eaten ashes like bread, and mingled my
drink with weeping, Because of thine indignation and
thy wrath: for thou hast lifted me up, and cast me down.
—PSALM 102:6–10

As the psalmist's troubles mounted, his hope dwindled to the point he felt he could not go on another day. Again, if you've not been in this desert place of discouragement, it seems unreasonable and unthinkable for others to linger. "Why don't they just move on?" you may wonder. Yet many of God's greatest servants—including David, a man after God's own heart—have found themselves stranded here in dark night seasons of the soul.

Like so many who have lost hope, David struggled to even know how to describe his feelings. With unusual metaphors, he sketched three images to delineate a portrait of his soul. First, he pictured a pelican in the wilderness, and he leaves the reader to question how this bird could survive so far from his usual sources of nourishment. Then, he relates to an owl of the desert, with its eerie wail and haunting stare. Finally, he turns to the common sparrow, this one mourning alone on the rooftop.

> *God's provisions, so radiantly seen in other seasons of our lives, are not limited by the dark.*

All three birds have a common denominator: they are alone. One of the most painful sensations in the desert of hopelessness is the feeling of lonely desolation. Somehow, it seems no one cares for you. Even in a large crowd of people, you can feel isolated from understanding.

So often in grief, it seems that everyone is against us. David felt taunted and defeated. He even felt that God was against him.

Could the night be darker? *Everything* seemed wrong for David. His health was failing, his emotional stamina was exhausted, and his hope was dry. The desert night was closing in on him.

NIGHTTIME PROVISIONS

Thankfully, even in desperate desolation, David knew where to turn. He poured out his soul to the Lord. When all seemed bleak, and he felt abandoned, he found comfort in the faithfulness of God.

God's provisions, so radiantly seen in other seasons of our lives, are not limited by the dark. Even in desert sunsets and the night that follows, He is there, and He will provide for our needs.

THE REALITY OF THE NIGHT

Have you noticed in the description above of David's sunsets how often the words *seemed* or *felt* occur? Feelings run strong in the night. But they don't necessarily reflect reality.

David made one of the greatest decisions one can make in the desert when he chose to express what he felt to the Lord but then focused on who God was and who He always will be.

In David's darkest moment, he remembered, "But thou, O LORD, shalt endure for ever; and thy remembrance unto all generations" (Psalm 102:12). There are three special comforts in the truth that God is everlasting.

GOD WILL NOT CHANGE

He has promised, "I am the LORD, I change not" (Malachi 3:6). And Hebrews 13:8 affirms, "Jesus Christ the same yesterday, and to day, and for ever." This means that every attribute we knew to be true of God before the night settled in, is still true. He does not love you less than He did before the desert sunset.

GOD WILL NOT FORGET US

In Isaiah 49:15–16, God asks, "Can a woman forget her sucking child, that she should not have compassion on the son of her womb? yea, they may forget, yet will I not forget thee. Behold, I have graven thee upon the palms of my hands; thy walls are continually before me." God loves His own through every age and every culture—to all generations.

GOD WILL NOT FORSAKE US

Even in desert nights, His promise stands, "I will never leave thee, nor forsake thee" (Hebrews 13:5).

Perhaps the greatest challenge of desert nights is to make deliberate choices to believe the promises of God above our feelings. When every emotion flooding our soul works to chisel a canyon of hopelessness, only deliberate faith in God can stem the tide and fill our lives with peace.

A DEFINING DECISION

On the tragic night when the Migliores lost their daughter Angie, I honestly didn't know what to say. As a very young pastor, I had never led people through an experience like this. I asked Dan if there was something specific for which I could pray for him. His response revealed the growth that had already been taking place in his own heart. "Pray that I will not let this make me bitter," he asked in a hoarse whisper.

We prayed together right then in the living room, and over the weeks and months that followed, I continued praying for the Migliore family to resist the temptation to bitterness. Their sweet love for the Lord and for others is, to this day, a testimony of the reality of God's grace in desert nights.

GOD'S VISIBLE HAND OF PROVISION

"During the first year and a half after our salvation, we learned a lot about God," Dan shared. "But through Angie's death, God taught us a lot about God's people, and more specifically, His institution—the local church."

As David poignantly expressed, those in a night season sometimes don't *feel* the reality of God's promises. God may seem distant and uninterested. Yet, God has ordained a special arm of provision for these times. He desires that His church would reach out to those members who are hurting and would communicate His love and care. Notes, a loving touch, perhaps a meal—all of these things are a visible manifestation of God's grace for the person who can't see the goodness of the Lord in the night.

The Lancaster Baptist Church family reached out to the Migliores in a way they desperately needed. God used dozens of people to help them carry their heavy burden. Initially, the love was expressed through meals, flowers, and cards. But even in the months that followed, our church family surrounded the Migliores with encouraging support.

Dan later said, "It was during that time in our life that I learned one of the most important lessons I have ever learned. The church is God's plan for keeping the body cared for and encouraged during difficult times."

FROM AN OPEN HAND TO AN OPEN HEART

For most of us, it's easier to be on the giving end of help than the receiving end. In speaking with Pennie while writing this chapter, one of her first comments was on the difficulty of receiving the help of others: "I'm the type of person who likes to go through things by myself without putting other people out or hurting someone else. It was difficult for me to even let people bring meals to the house. But a friend at church told us that we needed to let other people be a blessing to us."

Dan pointed out the not-so-pretty alternative to receiving help, "I have seen others go through similar trials, and the devil seems to find a way to destroy families that don't let their pastor and their church family minister to them." He is right. People who resist loving help alienate themselves from the provision

God is offering. Rather than surviving the desert night and finding the joy that comes in the morning, they wither in bitterness and eventually fall away.

God's provision can only sustain those who will receive it. When you're in the desert, stay connected to your church family. Be open with your pastor and others in the church who want to support you. Let God manifest His grace to you through His church.

SERVING THE PROVISIONS

The Migliores have gone full circle. Not only did they receive the help we offered them as a church, but they now give it to others. In describing the loss of Angie and the time that followed, Dan commented, "Over the next few years, I soon realized that God's plan is that sometimes *you* need the care and encouraging, and at other times, God wants to use you to provide the care that someone *else* may need." And I can attest that the Migliores provide the encouraging generously. Their own desert sunset has given them a tender heart for others walking in the dark.

This is part of the joy of being in a local church. God actually allows us to reveal His heart of love to others through acts of care.

Not only do we need the church to *receive* provision, but we need the church to *give* provision. As we are sensitive and responsive to the promptings of the Holy Spirit, we have the privilege of bringing God's light to desert nights.

PARADOXES IN THE DESERT

The Migliore's testimony reveals some of the most unique paradoxes of the Christian life: The God of light touches us in the darkness, and the omnipotent God strengthens us in weakness.

Regardless of our feelings, we truly are not like the owl in the desert or the lonely sparrow for whom no one cares. We are the children of the Heavenly Father, whose mercy endures forever and whose love is everlasting.

Whatever night you may be enduring, God wants you to see His love, care, and provision through His Word and through His local church. Like David, bring your needs to God, pour out your heart to Him, and He will sustain you. Psalm 55:22 says, "Cast thy burden upon the LORD, and he shall sustain thee: he shall never suffer the righteous to be moved."

BRILLIANT PROMISES

Desert sunsets are spectacular to behold. Airborne dust particles intensify the brilliant colors and add beauty to what might otherwise be a dismal signal of the coming night.

The declining seasons of our lives are similarly beautiful if we will but look to the brilliant promises of God. We so easily take God's promises for granted during the bright times. But when the shades of night steal over our souls, God's promises of faithfulness shine with greater resplendence.

The very consistency of the sunrise and the sunset are astounding reminders of God's great faithfulness. His faithfulness is as bright with the dawning of a new day as it is when the sun fades into a dusky goodnight. God never changes—He is always present, and He is always faithful.

So, what can you do when the night closes in around you and discouragement sets in? Trust God's promises. Focus on the reality of who God is rather than how you feel or what seems to be true. Stay inseparably connected to your church. And, when the morning comes, you will see the beauty that God worked in your life through the desert night.

DESERT PARTICIPATION
WHEN GOD MULTIPLIES HIS GIFTS

N ahum and Nora Galdamez were noticeably uncomfortable as we met at the restaurant. This was the first time Terrie and I personally met this couple who regularly attended our Spanish services, and our lunch appointment was prompted by a difficult circumstance.

A few days earlier, our school principal had explained to me in a staff meeting that he had to expel three students from our Christian school—the Galdamez' daughter included. Because our Christian school is sponsored by the church, I have the opportunity and privilege to pastor our students, faculty, and parents through some of these more difficult times. In the case of these three students being expelled, the Lord laid on my heart to ask some pastoral staff members to each take one of these families to lunch in order to let them know that we loved them and that we were there to help them restore their children into a right relationship with God and ultimately return to Lancaster Baptist School, should they desire.

Personally, I chose to take the Galdamez family, who agreed, rather reluctantly, to have lunch with us. At first, the conversation was a little stiff, as we briefly discussed the situation of the school. Then we expressed our love and desire to help, and the Lord's grace was evident as we developed a wonderful friendship.

A few days later, Nahum asked if he could have lunch again with me sometime. We agreed to meet at the same restaurant the following week. At the time, my schedule was exceptionally busy, and squeezing in the time seemed difficult. I had no idea, however, of what was about to happen in that meeting.

MISSION IMPOSSIBLE

Have you ever been given a job that was beyond your ability to complete? The kind of assignment that would be impossible to accomplish even if you engaged every resource within your power?

Such was the belief concerning space exploration many years ago. It seemed unrealistic to even fathom man personally visiting and discovering space. Not any longer, however. Thanks to the diligent efforts and meticulous skill of scientists, NASA has launched many successful missions into space.

Much of the research for these missions takes place at the Dryden Research Center, which is situated within Edward's Air Force Base right here in the Mojave Desert. The open space for flights and the relatively mild weather year round make the desert a superb place for aeronautical research.

Several years ago, I had the opportunity to tour the Dryden center. I was amazed as I watched highly skilled engineers testing and developing some of the most advanced instruments in the world. The entire tour was an impressive reminder of the skill and intelligence invested into space exploration.

God actually delights in giving impossible assignments.

But, assuming you are not an astronaut, can you imagine personally being thrust into a space shuttle and directed to oversee one of these outer space missions? That would be Mission Impossible!

This may surprise you, but God actually delights in giving impossible assignments. In fact, the central mission of the church is such an assignment:

> *Go ye therefore, and teach all nations, baptizing them in the name of the Father, and of the Son, and of the Holy Ghost: Teaching them to observe all things whatsoever I have commanded you: and, lo, I am with you alway, even unto the end of the world. Amen.*
> —MATTHEW 28:19–20

God has given us a mission that reaches far beyond our current position, and far beyond our human ability. Frankly, it's impossible.

But the God who specializes in the impossible prefaced His command with the wonderful declaration, "All power is given unto me in heaven and in earth" (Matthew 28:18). The desert places of our lives provide excellent opportunities to discover the limitless power of God and a chance to see the impossible accomplished.

DESERT ASSIGNMENTS

All four gospels record one particularly startling impossible assignment Jesus gave His disciples, and it happened to be in the desert.

Jesus had brought the disciples with Him to this remote location seeking solitude and rest from the demands of a busy schedule and the drain of continually serving. But as the group attempted to slip away from the crowd, they were spotted.

Jesus told His disciples to do something that they didn't have the resources to do.

No sooner had they reached the desert when thousands flocked to join them. Jesus, moved with compassion, set His own needs for rest aside and healed their sick and taught the multitude.

As the sun began to set, the disciples were ready to call it a day. "Send the multitude away," they suggested, "that they may go into the villages, and buy themselves victuals" (Matthew 14:15).

But Jesus had a different answer to the dilemma. He had an assignment for the disciples: "They need not depart; give ye them to eat" (Matthew 14:16).

Now, this was no small group. Scripture specifically records there were five thousand men, not counting women and children. If each man had a wife and just one child, the crowd would have been fifteen thousand people, and it was quite possibly much larger.

How could twelve men provide food for this crowd? Impossible. Too big. Not even a chance.

I can just see the disciples gulp and look at each other in disbelief. Did Jesus really just tell *them* to feed all those people?

Yes, Jesus absolutely told His disciples to do something that they didn't have the resources to do. This was a desert place assignment. Like the desert in which they stood or the sea of people by which they were surrounded, it looked vast, unending, no way to even begin.

CALCULATIONS

Philip regained his senses first. He cleared his throat and in a steady voice, slowly explained to Jesus why they *couldn't* feed the people. "Two hundred pennyworth of bread is not sufficient for them, that every one of them may take a little" (John 6:7). It didn't take a NASA mathematician to figure that one out!

Philip's response was the same as many of ours when we're faced with a desert assignment. He calculated how far they could go with human resources, realized these weren't sufficient, and suggested they skip the whole project altogether.

But Jesus was trying to retrain the disciples' thinking. Yes, a desert assignment is too big for *us*. But it's not too big for *God*. In fact, a desert assignment is actually a God-sized opportunity. It is a chance to participate in something so great, that only God could do it.

THE RESOURCES TO ACCOMPLISH A DESERT MISSION

If you were surprised to learn that God delights in assigning impossible tasks, you may be even more surprised to realize that He uses our insufficient resources to do it.

Like Philip, we think that unless there is some large reservoir of resources of which we were unaware, there's no hope for success. God, however, uses and supernaturally blesses what we already possess to get His work accomplished.

For instance, God used the rod in the hand of Moses to part the Red Sea, the sling in the hand of David to fell a giant, and the pitcher, lamp, and trumpet in the hand of Gideon to defeat the Midianites.

So when Jesus wanted to feed thousands of people in the desert, He did it with the resources at hand:

> And they say unto him, We have here but five loaves, and two fishes. He said, Bring them hither to me. And he commanded the multitude to sit down on the grass, and took the five loaves, and the two fishes, and looking up to heaven, he blessed, and brake, and gave the loaves to his disciples, and the disciples to the multitude. And they did all eat, and were filled: and they took up of the fragments that remained twelve baskets full.
> —MATTHEW 14:17–20

God can take our small and insignificant resources and with them accomplish more than is humanly possible.

DIVINE MATH

If we were to reduce our approach to success into mathematical terms, our formula would look something like this:

> Assignment
> + My resources
> _____
> Mission accomplished

By our formula, if "assignment" is too great or "my resources" are too small, then obviously the mission can't be accomplished.

God's formula, however, for calculating success is different:

> Assignment
> + My resources given to God
> x God's intervention
> _____
> Mission accomplished

THE DECIDING FACTOR

We all have resources. But none of us have great enough resources to see a desert assignment accomplished. So how is it that some people's resources are multiplied and other's aren't?

Here's the deciding factor: God only multiplies the resources that we give to Him. Many Christians never see God multiply their resources because they never give their resources to God.

I've seen many Christians protect and hoard their resources. *After all,* they reason, *the comparatively little I could contribute*

wouldn't make a difference anyway. I may as well enjoy it myself.
But every time I've seen people freely and cheerfully give to God,
I've seen Him bless and multiply in a phenomenal way.

PARTICIPATION—A GIFT

Our opportunity to give to God is actually His gift to us. It is the
gift of participation.

Think about it. Jesus didn't need the boy's lunch to feed
the multitude. Anyone who can take five loaves and two fish
and feed in excess of five thousand people with it, could just as
easily feed them without the meager lunch. But by accepting
the lunch, Jesus gave this boy the joy of being part of something
much bigger than he could have accomplished on his own.

Jesus gave the disciples the same opportunity when He
told them to organize the people and distribute the bread: "And
Jesus said, Make the men sit down. Now there was much grass in
the place. So the men sat down, in number about five thousand.
And Jesus took the loaves; and when he had given thanks, he
distributed to the disciples, and the disciples to them that were
set down; and likewise of the fishes as much as they would"
(John 6:10–11).

Again, Christ could have handled this whole meal without
the disciples' help. He could have distributed the food by
supernatural means, just as He had miraculously multiplied it.
But He gave the disciples the gift of participation.

Desert assignments are our opportunities to participate in
God's work—to know the joy of involvement in something so
much bigger than ourselves.

A GREATER OPPORTUNITY

The Lord knew that in one year from the time He fed the five thousand, He would ascend into Heaven. Once again, the disciples would be responsible to "pass the bread," only this time, it would be the Bread of Life!

We already saw Matthew 28:19–20 where Jesus told His disciples to reach the world with the Gospel. We call it the Great Commission. How could twelve men—twelve fearful men—bring the Gospel to the entire world—a hostile world? Impossible. Too big. Not even a chance.

But they did it. Colossians 1:6 records that the first-century church spread the Gospel "in all the world."

By the time Christ gave the Great Commission, the disciples had learned how desert assignments work. They put their resources—their time, their money, their voices, even their lives—at Jesus' disposal and simply obeyed His directions. He multiplied their efforts, and the rest is history.

OUR MISSION

The Great Commission of Matthew 28:19–20 hasn't changed. We, too, are assigned to bring the Gospel to the entire world—in this generation.

Impossible? Yes! Too big? Absolutely.

That is why Jesus promised, "But ye shall receive power, after that the Holy Ghost is come upon you: and ye shall be witnesses unto me both in Jerusalem, and in all Judaea, and in Samaria, and unto the uttermost part of the earth" (Acts 1:8).

This desert assignment is only possible through the power of God. And it is only realized when we put ourselves at His disposal. Then He multiplies our meager resources and propels our efforts to regions far beyond what we could do on our own.

AN UNUSUAL OFFER

I wasn't sure what to expect at my next lunch meeting with Nahum Galdamez. We met at the restaurant and ordered our food. As we ate, he made an incredible offer.

Brother Galdamez had immigrated to the States from El Salvador, and much of his family still lived in his home country. He told me he had inherited a school back in El Salvador, and then he requested, "Would you consider going to El Salvador with me to see the school firsthand? Maybe our church could help bring the Gospel to the students there."

You'd think I'd jump at an opportunity like that, and, looking back, I'm surprised that I didn't. But for some reason, it didn't really make sense to me. I promised Nahum that I'd think about it, but warned that I didn't think I could go.

But Nahum Galdamez wasn't a man to be easily deterred. A day or two after our lunch meeting, he arrived at my office and presented me with a photo album containing pictures of the school in El Salvador. "Pastor," he pleaded, "would you please consider coming with me to see for yourself?"

In the next several minutes, he described how he had come to America and began working at a trucking company for $2.50 an hour while he dreamed of someday owning his own truck and perhaps even his own company.

Ever since he arrived in America, he had been giving at least 20 percent of his income to the Lord. The Lord had blessed, and he now owned several trucks and a growing trucking company.

As I looked through the photo album and listened to his story, Nahum explained that he would like to underwrite the trip to El Salvador if we would just be willing to go.

POWER IN ACTION

A few months after Nahum brought me the photo album, I was on a plane seated next to him flying to the tiny country of El Salvador. Days earlier, a few members of Lancaster Baptist Church and a small team of West Coast Baptist College students had gone before us to prepare for the services we would hold and to invite El Salvadorians to the services. Little did we know what God had in store.

Upon arrival, we settled briefly into a hotel room and got ready for the evening service. We made our way to the city of Cojutepeque where it was agreed that I would preach in the auditorium of the school. Amazingly, the meeting was nationally televised and, as the result of those who had gone ahead of us, several hundred people gathered to hear the preaching that night.

By the grace of God, many accepted Jesus as their Saviour, and after the service, I had the privilege of leading Nahum's cousin to Christ. His cousin is the chief of police in San Salvador.

The next day, we went to the northern town of Metapán. As we looked around the town, we walked into a beautiful restaurant overlooking a lake in the city just south of the

Honduras border. At the restaurant, we had the opportunity to meet the owner, who was also running for mayor of the city.

The Lord impressed upon my heart to ask him if he knew for sure that Heaven would be his home some day. He indicated he was not sure, so I asked if he might give us a little time to share the Gospel with him. He listened intently through an interpreter and, some time later, accepted Jesus Christ as his Saviour.

Throughout the few days in the country, God was moving in such an unusual way. I knew that my meeting with Nahum was something that had been ordained of God.

RESOURCES MULTIPLIED

After returning to the States, one of the young men on the trip indicated to me that he felt the Lord had called him to El Salvador to be a missionary. Soon, another family felt God call them to this field as well.

A few months later, we resumed a new school year at Lancaster Baptist School. The Galdamez's daughter, Eunice, was back in school, and, in fact, in the early months of the school year accepted Christ as her Saviour.

Since Brother Galdamez' offer to give his inheritance (the school in El Salvador) to the Lord, God has done far more than we could have dreamed. We have now sent three missionaries to El Salvador, two churches have been established (one meeting in the restaurant the mayor owned), and souls are being saved on a weekly basis. The Lord has allowed us, on numerous occasions, to have teams visit the country and conduct crusades during which many people have been saved. The school is now the home of Emmanuel Baptist Church, and it is operating daily, ministering to children in Kindergarten through the twelfth grade in this needy area.

OPPORTUNITY UNLIMITED

The fact that God allows us to have a part in His work never ceases to amaze me. Even as I give everything within me to the Lord, I feel like a small boy sitting next to an astronaut in the cockpit of a space shuttle. He tells me which levers to pull and which buttons to push. As I follow His instructions, I get to be in on something I could never do on my own.

What is the desert assignment you are facing right now? What do you know God wants you to do, but you hesitate because you don't have the resources?

Remember God's formula for success:

> Assignment
> + My resources given to God
> x God's intervention
> _____
> Mission accomplished

Give your all to God. He still works miracles in desert places.

TWELVE

DESERT PATHS
WHERE CHOICES ARE MADE

L uis Montaño was not unlike many of the teenagers involved in our city gangs in the 1990s. He came to church with a shaved head and baggy pants, but underneath his tough exterior was a young man with a troubled past.

Luis was born in Hermosillo, Mexico. His parents were divorced when he was six years old. His mother feared that his father would use his political influence to take Luis and his two sisters away from her, so she moved the family to Lancaster, California.

The family lived about two miles from Lancaster Baptist Church, and soulwinners often knocked on their door. Mrs. Montaño, however, was a Catholic and consistently sent them away. Luis sometime made fun of them with his friends.

As a teen, Luis struggled. He got involved in a gang, and his grades plummeted. His lifestyle brought him to four different high schools, and when he eventually graduated, it was from a continuation school.

A family he met invited Luis to Open House Sunday in 1996. This time, he accepted the invitation. Little did that family know why.

A godly usher noticed Luis as he slipped into one of the back pews of the Spanish department and listened to the service. As the message closed, our Spanish pastor invited anyone who did not know Christ as Saviour to come to the front where someone would show them from the Bible how to be saved.

The usher tapped Luis on the shoulder. "I noticed you're visiting today. Let me ask you a question: If you were to die today, are you 100 percent sure that you would spend eternity in Heaven?"

Too proud to admit he needed salvation, Luis responded, "I believe in God. I'm not really interested."

In reality, Luis was intensely interested.

Three months prior, Luis had been at a late night party when a thirteen-year-old boy pulled out a sawed-off shotgun and shot into the crowd near where Luis was standing. Luis couldn't sleep that night, or the next. In fact, ever since, he often wondered, "What if I were on the other side of that barrel?"

SEEKING FOR DIRECTION

The desert is a land of many paths. Dusty trails, winding between the sagebrush and through desert canyons, carry travelers through arid wastelands. Some paths are proven to lead to water and protection. Others meander aimlessly to more expanses of nothing.

If we were to liken lifestyle choices to paths in the desert, it's obvious the world doesn't know the way. They wander down paths filled with pleasure but ending in emptiness and dissatisfaction.

Teenagers like Luis find acceptance in gangs and a measure of relief from fear in drugs. Some people plunge into debt as they seek for a path of fulfillment in possessions. Many feed the coffers of the entertainment industry as they attempt to avoid reality and traverse a path of amusement. Others find the path of internet addictions.

God has given us, His people, the privilege to minister in a day when the world is desperate for answers.

God has given us, His people, the privilege to minister in a day when the world is desperate for answers. As people all around us are obviously struggling to find a path of satisfaction and fulfillment, God has given us the opportunity to point all of these people down the path of truth—the path to the Lord Jesus Christ who is "the way, the truth, and the life" (John 14:6).

There's just one problem. God's people seem to have lost the way.

Churches across the nation are abandoning the old paths of biblical ministry and following popular culture down paths of worldliness. Amazingly, they believe that if the church moves to the path of the ungodly, she can better call the ungodly off the path.

The prophet Jeremiah lived in a day when his people were making the wrong choices of spiritual desert paths. Although they had seen firsthand the incredible guidance of God and known the joy of walking with Him, they were now choosing to go their own way—preferring paths of greater immediate attraction to the old and proven paths of righteousness.

What the Israelites didn't realize is that the paths they were choosing led to destruction and a certain national calamity. God sent Jeremiah to warn His people and to call them to return to the old and proven paths of blessing: "Thus saith the LORD, Stand ye in the ways, and see, and ask for the old paths, where is the good way, and walk therein, and ye shall find rest for your souls. But they said, We will not walk therein" (Jeremiah 6:16).

As to Judah of old, God still calls His people to return to the old paths.

CROSSROADS

As Jeremiah sounded out God's call to His people, he painted an image of a desert traveler who has arrived at a point where the trail divides into several paths. Now this traveler must make a choice. Which way to go?

God's first piece of counsel is to stand and consider. He is challenging His people to make a responsible, conscious choice rather than simply rushing on to the path that appears the most pleasant, comfortable, or promising. He counsels them to contemplate the crossroads rather than hastily bypassing a decision.

As they pause, God directs His people to "see"—to observe the characteristics of the path in question. Is it a proven path, marked by the footprints of God's blessing? Or is it a destructive path, with the edges blurred and exact direction unclear?

When we step back and look at the paths many churches today are taking, we see some startling characteristics. Like hazardous canyon trails in the desert, they wind dangerously near the world and wander around fleshly attractions. They are landmarked with a lack of distinctive living, a loss of doctrinal integrity, and a decline in spiritual commitment.

If a teenager like Luis Montaño were to visit many churches in America today, he would be greeted by a youth pastor who looked like he was trying to imitate Luis' gang friends, hear music that could have been taken right off of Luis' iPod (with the words adjusted slightly), and hear a message lacking any solid truth or biblical moorings. He would encounter nothing that would point him to seriously consider his present path and make a decision for Christ. He would leave exactly as he came— still desperate for a different direction.

ASK FOR THE OLD PATHS

As the traveler in Jeremiah's picture has observed the choices before him, God now counsels him to ask for directions before he makes his choice.

But he must be careful in how he phrases his question. If he asks, "Which way should I go?" he'll get answers directing him down a multitude of paths. Church growth experts will jump at the opportunity to influence his decision. Blog writers will fill his media stream with ideas and "tricks" to gain a crowd. The world itself will answer his surveys with what they would like to find in a church—of course, they would rule out conviction-producing preaching. And all the answers would sound plausible and appealing.

But, if as he stands considering directions, he asks, "Which of these is the old path?" he will be directed to the proven methods of Scripture—what Jeremiah calls "the good way."

People today say the old paths don't work. They say that the old paths are anti-cultural and don't reach our generation. If by "old path" one means avoiding technology and using outdated materials, then perhaps they are correct in their conclusion. But if by "old path" one simply means walking and ministering according to principles of holiness and faithfulness to God's Word, they are mistaken. The old path is the good way.

One of the reasons I'm thankful for what God has done here in Lancaster is that it proves that the old paths still work. Our church started with a handful of people on the backside of the desert. We printed tracts and began going soulwinning. We loved people and preached the truth. We discipled new converts and encouraged growth in grace. And it worked.

We had no rock band concerts, no seeker-driven community surveys, no worldly styled entertainment. We just followed the old paths.

God took a struggling church in the middle of the desert who determined to walk in the old paths, and He blessed it. The old paths are still the good way.

Pastor, you don't need new "tricks" to build your church. You need the old paths of soulwinning, compassion, and Spirit-filled preaching and discipleship.

Christian, if you are in a church walking in the old paths, thank God for it! Refuse the tendency to veer off to a path leading to seemingly greener plants. Whole-heartedly invest yourself in teaming with your church to do God's work in God's way.

COMMITMENT TO CONTINUE

"But," you might ask, "if the old path is the good way, why isn't everyone using it?"

The old path is the good way because it ends at a good destination. But it's not the easy way. The old path is sometimes steep, and dusty, and tiring, and even lonely. And some people prefer the immediate results of easier trails, little recognizing that the easy trails fail to produce lasting spiritual fruit.

Statistics are revealing the barrenness of the seeker-sensitive church model of the last decades. Young people especially are bailing out of church in high percentages. Most churches are losing over 70 percent of their young people once they graduate high school, and many never return. The new paths may help gather a crowd, but they take the crowd in the wrong direction.

Our nation is in desperate need for revival. Even as Jeremiah ministered in a time of spiritual unfaithfulness and idolatry, so America today is rapidly turning from God. Americans are increasingly refusing the faith of our fathers and insisting on a path of self-destruction through moral decline and a rejection of truth.

How can we call the nation back to the good way if we ourselves are forsaking the old paths? We need pastors and people who will trust God's Word—that God will bless the old paths—and who will commit to "walk therein."

Yes, the old path is rigorous. But it leads to an incredible destination. Lancaster Baptist Church is one of thousands of churches around the world that proves that a church committed to the old paths can lead people down a road of grace that brings even unlikely people in unlikely places to a life-changing encounter with God.

PATH OF REST

God makes an incredible promise concerning the old paths: "ye shall find rest for your souls" (Jeremiah 6:16). The old path provides deep and satisfying soul rest—the kind of rest that can only come by a direct relationship with Jesus Christ.

So many today have a weary soul because they are on the wrong path.

Even as a sixteen year old, Luis Montaño knew the burden of a weary soul. His past was more troubled than the usher who attempted to share the Gospel with him knew. Deep in his soul he craved rest. And this hunger was so strong that it drew him back to church the following Sunday.

All week long, Luis thought about the usher's question: "If you were to die today, are you 100 percent sure that you would spend eternity in Heaven?" He could hardly wait for the next Sunday. When he got to church, he quickly found the usher who had asked him about his salvation.

"Sir," he began, "you asked me a question last week, and I really want to know the answer to it today."

The usher gladly sat down with Luis and showed him from the Bible how he could be saved. Then he encouraged Luis to receive Christ as his Saviour.

"No," Luis protested. "This is way too simple. There is no way that everything I've done could be simply forgiven. It's just too easy."

The usher tried to convince Luis that Jesus' sacrifice is truly sufficient to pay for all of his sin. But Luis couldn't see it. The rest he so desperately craved surely couldn't be that simply attained.

The family who first invited Luis to church invited him to their home for dinner that afternoon. At the table, Luis asked a question that had been burning in his heart all morning. Disguising his intensity, he casually asked, "By the way, what do you think about salvation?" With joy, they opened the Bible and showed Luis the plan of salvation.

Finally, Luis understood that, although receiving salvation is simple for us, Jesus paid a great price for it. That night, Luis asked Christ to save him. And from that moment on, Luis was on a different path.

PATH OF PERSEVERANCE

Luis grew by leaps and bounds. Immediately, he displayed a hunger for things of the Lord and a determination to press forward.

A few weeks after salvation, Luis was baptized. I didn't learn until years later, as Luis gave his testimony in church, what difficulty Luis had in getting baptized, or his remarkable solution.

Because he was still under eighteen, we required that one of his parents sign a permission slip for him to be baptized. Luis brought the slip home and asked his mom to sign. A staunch Catholic, she refused. He asked again the next week. She refused again.

Luis was desperate. He knew Christ had changed his life, and he really wanted to follow Him in believer's baptism. Then, Luis had an idea. *None of the people at the church know what my mother's signature looks like. I'll just sign her name myself.* He did, and he was baptized! (His mother has since been saved and is a faithful member of our church.)

Six months after Luis was saved, he came to me at the end of the service with a big smile and an important announcement. "Pastor, I feel God has called me to preach."

I was thrilled! But before I could respond, he continued, "Do you know of any good Bible colleges where I could train?"

At that point, I thought he was playing some kind of a prank. After all, as the president of West Coast Baptist College, I had done my best to make sure our young people knew that they could attend Bible college right on our eighty-acre campus. I looked into Luis' eyes and said, "Well, it just so happens we have a Bible college right here called West Coast Baptist College."

He surprised me again when he responded by sincerely asking for more information about the school. The following semester, Luis enrolled and began training at West Coast Baptist College.

Amazingly, this young man who had so struggled in high school, began to excel in his college studies. He worked diligently and gave himself to learn and grow.

Luis' appetite for ministry was insatiable. He helped serve in our Spanish youth department, the bus ministry, and other outreach programs. It was obvious that Luis was set on following the good way.

NEW BEGINNINGS ON THE OLD PATH

Through helping in the Spanish ministry, Luis met Magdalena Sandoval, a young lady who had also accepted Christ through our ministry. Luis and Maggie fell in love, and it was my privilege to conduct their wedding ceremony.

After graduating from West Coast Baptist College and getting married, the couple moved to the San Jose area where they began serving full time in the ministry. Luis' responsibilities included overseeing and preaching in the Spanish department of the church, helping with outreach ministries, and overseeing graphic design.

A couple of years later, Lancaster Baptist Church had the privilege of ordaining Luis into the Gospel ministry. As the pastoral staff and deacons met with Luis and began questioning him regarding his doctrine and philosophy of ministry, we were truly amazed at what God had done in his life. All of us in the meeting wept as we listened to him recount his story.

As he shared how God transformed him from a troubled teenager to a preacher of the Gospel, we realized anew the power of the Gospel and the fruitfulness of local church ministry. His biblical answers to the questions regarding Bible doctrine were astounding. Often, he would answer using the Greek he learned in college and the Hebrew he had taught himself over the last two years. He shared his vision to go to the mission field and establish a church like the church that reached him, as well as a Bible college to train others in church planting.

After a few years of ministry in San Jose, Luis was among the young men who went to El Salvador with me (see chapter 11 for the story of this trip). I felt pretty sure that Luis would surrender his heart to the field of El Salvador. He knew the language. He had told me he had a great desire for missions, and there were so many doors opening in El Salvador at the time. I was a little surprised as we were flying home when Luis came up to my seat to see me. "Pastor Chappell, this trip has meant so much to me. After visiting El Salvador, I know that God has called me to Mexico to be a missionary!"

Several months later, Luis returned home to Lancaster Baptist Church and began deputation. He began calling pastors across the country and setting up meetings to present his work and raise financial support. With the same diligence and persistence he had demonstrated in Bible college, Luis raised his support in record-setting time. He once told me that he would rise at 5:00 AM and begin making phone calls at 6:00 AM to the pastors on the East coast. He called well over two thousand churches simply to line up meetings in a few hundred churches. His passion to get to the field was amazing.

PATH OF BLESSING

I remember a few years ago when Luis called me and said, "Pastor, we are getting ready to drive across the border at Nogales.

Pray that things will go well." Things did go well at the border crossing, and they have been going well ever since.

Luis is now the pastor of the Hermosillo Baptist Church in his birth town. He and Maggie are winning souls to Christ on a weekly basis, discipling them, and building a local New Testament Baptist Church.

Luis' story speaks of the fulfillment of the old paths. Because Lancaster Baptist Church was faithful to walk in the old paths, God used us to reach Luis and see his life transformed. Today, Luis is directing Mexicans to the old paths of rest and service.

I'm thankful we didn't abandon the old paths.

WHERE CHOICES ARE MADE

An intersection of paths leaves the traveler with a choice. Perhaps you're standing at such an intersection weighing your options. You can shift to an alternate path, perhaps an easier or more popular path. Or you can take another step forward on the good path, the old path.

When God presented this choice to the Israelites and pleaded with them to walk in the old paths, they responded, "We will not walk therein" (Jeremiah 6:16). Pushing past the warnings of their weeping prophet, they plunged ahead on the path of pleasure and idolatry. And they suffered the consequences—seventy years in foreign captivity.

America today is suffering the consequences of pastors and churches who have refused the old paths. Where we should have been calling our nation back to God and to righteousness, we've instead been obsessed with drawing large crowds and becoming visibly successful. We've traded the steep paths of preaching the Gospel and loving people for the easy ways of fitting in and comforting people.

The stories in this book are a testimony to the fact that the old paths really do work. Even in the context of twenty-first century ministry, God still blesses the basic principles of His Word. God's grace is powerful! And seeing it in action doesn't require jumping paths to manufacture a semblance of God's blessing. He still transforms lives by the power of the Gospel and the ministry of the local church. I'm thankful our church has chosen to seek the old paths.

What choices lie before you? Are you feeling pressured to stray from the old paths, to choose an alternate route? Ask for the old paths, and continue to walk in it when the way gets dusty and you get weary.

The old path is the good path. It leads to God Himself, the living water. It leads to rest and peace. Choose the old paths—where God blesses in desert places.

THIRTEEN

DESERT ROSES
WHY THE DESERT BLOSSOMS

L eo Walther was fifty-seven years old when he first came to Lancaster Baptist Church, and he wasn't there because he had a hunger for truth.

For thirty years, Leo had been in the liquor business, owning a liquor convenience store in Sunland, a rural suburb of Los Angeles. The business had flourished, and his diligent and loyal employees did most of the work. In fact, Leo often played five games of golf a week.

When Leo sold the business and retired at fifty-one, he was actually bored. He played more golf and traveled with his wife, Evelyn, but other than that, his life was becoming pretty empty.

DESERT BLOSSOMS

The classic desert site is Death Valley. Amazingly, this valley that sustains the highest temperatures in North America also features an occasional spectacular wildflower bloom. Seas of gold, purple, pink, or white blossoms ripple across the desert for a few short weeks until the blistering heat kills the delicate blossoms.

The blossoms are the fruit of seeds that have quietly waited in the desert soil until they receive enough rain. Then they erupt into a beautiful display—proof that even the desert can sustain life.

To be sure, this stunning display occurs rarely—and only under perfect conditions. There must be just so much sun and evenly spaced rain in sufficient quantities over the fall and winter months. Then, when the conditions are met, the desert comes alive with color and beauty.

THE BLOSSOM EFFECT

Isaiah 35 transports us to a time when the desert places of the Middle East will likewise blossom with profuse color and immense beauty. During the millennial reign of Christ, refreshing waves will break out, and the desert—the dry, empty, barren wastelands—will revive and blossom as a rose.

Although this passage points to the future (after the Rapture, Tribulation, and Second Coming of Christ), it also describes the necessary conditions for spiritual blossoms in the desert. Where the conditions presented in this chapter are prevalent today, desert ministry can blossom in surprising displays of beauty. The hardest hearts and driest lives can be transformed into fragrant exhibits of God's grace.

So what conditions produce desert roses?

ABUNDANT WATER

Typical desert blossoms sprout from plants that are hardy to heat and drought and are able to survive on minimal water. But Isaiah 35 speaks of a time when streams of refreshing water will saturate the ground, and the entire desert will blossom with life and vitality. The blossoms here reflect a miracle.

To fully communicate the dearth previous to this miracle, God uses a threefold description emphasizing the desert's barrenness: "The *wilderness* and the *solitary place* shall be glad for them; and the *desert* shall rejoice, and blossom as the rose" (Isaiah 35:1, emphasis added). This verse does not simply describe a location that's been a bit short on rainfall recently. It describes a harsh, violent, wasteland that is dry and thirsty. Yet even here, the Word of the Lord makes a difference.

All of us anticipate fruit in well-watered, richly fertilized lives—hearts where conditions are perfect for spiritual growth. But even in unlikely places with unlikely people, sweet desert blossoms proclaim the power of God's Word.

Desert ministry is the opportunity to channel God's Word to barren and wasted lives.

Isaiah 55:10–11 likens God's Word to water, and it pictures the ability it has to turn hearts toward the Lord: "For as the rain cometh down, and the snow from heaven, and returneth not thither, but watereth the earth, and maketh it bring forth and bud, that it may give seed to the sower, and bread to the eater: So shall my word be that goeth forth out of my mouth: it shall not return unto me void, but it shall accomplish that which I please, and it shall prosper in the thing whereto I sent it."

Desert ministry is the opportunity to channel God's Word to barren and wasted lives.

RUN-OFF

The Lord had already given Leo the opportunity to be the recipient of desert ministry—primarily through his wife, Evelyn.

Evelyn had been saved as a child, and she went to church every Sunday, bringing their three children with her until they left the house. For Evelyn's sake, Leo even paid for the children to receive their education in a Christian school. But Leo wasn't one bit interested in church, and he sure had no intention of being saved. Like water run-off on the desert surface, Leo dismissed Evelyn's godly influence.

OBLIGATING OPPORTUNITY

Through the years, Evelyn prayed for Leo and did all she could to encourage their children to live for the Lord. Shortly after their son and daughter-in-law, Craig and Lorriane, moved to Lancaster for Craig's job, Evelyn noticed an ad in the *Sword of the Lord* for Lancaster Baptist Church.

The couple was not in church at the time, but Lorriane had recently been showing some interest in church. From the ad Evelyn saw, she thought our church would be helpful to

Lorriane. Evelyn offered to drive up to Lancaster to attend with her for her first visit.

Just a few days later, Craig called Evelyn. "Mom, how would you like to keep the kids on Saturday? They could spend the night with you, and then you could bring them back to Lancaster Sunday morning and meet us at church? Some men from that church you were telling us about came by and invited me. I told them our whole family would be there this Sunday."

Two soulwinners from our church had obtained Craig and Lorriane's address as new move-ins to the community. They stopped by the house with a welcome packet for the Antelope Valley as well as a warm invitation to our church.

> *Our greatest energy is invested in watering our desert blossoms with God's Word through teaching, preaching, and discipleship.*

Evelyn was delighted! Leo, however, wasn't. As he had told Evelyn before, he felt like a hypocrite going to church because of the business he owned.

"But we really need to support our children in this," she nudged.

Somewhat grudgingly, Leo rose early Sunday morning and drove Evelyn and their two grandchildren to meet Craig and Lorriane at church. An usher greeted the family and seated them directly in front of the pulpit.

Leo was a gracious man and didn't let on how much he disliked being in church. But before I even began the sermon, he had closed his heart to the Gospel message. He wasn't what you would think of as a likely candidate for salvation.

IRRIGATION SYSTEMS

Desert farming is only possible with the use of irrigation—applying water to the soil. Even so, we must channel God's life-giving truth to parched hearts through the preaching and teaching of His Word. God saves people through "the foolishness of preaching" (1 Corinthians 1:21).

From the earliest days of my ministry, I determined that every sermon would be so thoroughly saturated with God's Word that even if I failed in articulating the message through *my* words, hearers would still be able to drink deeply from the wells of Scripture. This means that I must be diligent in spending time studying for my messages. If they are to be full of Scripture, I can't pull a topic out of a hat, attach three points and verses to it, and then spend thirty minutes "winging it" in the pulpit. My highest priority each week in leading our church is to prepare a life-changing, Scripture-filled message.

Additionally, we've determined to make God's Word central in every ministry of our church. In youth activities, singles events, couples retreats, senior outings—every ministry is centered on helping people immerse their lives in biblical truths. We encourage fellowship and sponsor activities, but we use these to nurture hearts for God and encourage a hunger for spiritual growth. Our greatest energy is invested in watering our desert blossoms with God's Word through teaching, preaching, and discipleship.

ARTIFICIAL FLOWERS

Because God has given us His Word as the primary irrigation system for desert growth, we can have confidence in using it— even when it appears to be less effective than other methods. Through the years, I've observed that any growth that takes place apart from the Word of God produces artificial flowers.

It is possible to cultivate an *appearance* of growth that turns out to be lacking reality. It is possible to promote a spirit of excitement that is nothing more than a feeling. It is possible to facilitate religious experiences that are zealous in nature, but empty in substance. As time passes and the excitement wears, it becomes evident that these methods produce no true life change.

Don't get me wrong. Desert ministry is exciting! There is no thrill like using God's Word to lead a soul to Christ and then, through consistent watering with Scripture, seeing that person blossom into a fruitful Christian. I'm passionate about desert ministry, and I thank God for the spirit of excitement and joy our church has in delivering God's Word to others.

But when it comes to authentic growth or artificial blossoms, the only consistent delineator between the two is the quality of the irrigation system. How much of the process is centered on applying God's Word to thirsty hearts?

DESERT TRANSFORMATION

When Leo Walther came to Lancaster Baptist Church, his life was truly a wasteland, devoured by years of an unholy occupation and now empty of substance or joy. He had allowed the bits of water that could have reached him through his wife to run off his barren heart and be lost as he chased vain pursuits.

He sat in church on that Sunday morning with his heart closed and his mind set. But as I preached, Craig and Lorriane listened carefully. During the invitation, they both walked to the front and were saved.

Once again, Evelyn was thrilled. And as she and Leo drove back home, she ventured to ask, "How did you like it?"

"Friendliest place I've ever been," Leo acknowledged. "I've never felt so welcomed at a church before." He hesitated, "but I'm not going back. The preacher was too loud."

Leo and Evelyn did go back, however, because the following Wednesday Craig and Lorriane were baptized. Once again, Evelyn convinced Leo that they needed to go support their children. And once again, Leo grudgingly sat with his heart closed and his mind set.

But he returned the following Sunday, and the next, and the next. As Leo continued to hear the preaching of God's Word, his heart began to soften. The Holy Spirit convicted him of his condition and convinced him of his need for Christ.

Finally, one Sunday morning, Craig nudged his dad during the invitation. Together, they went to the front, and Leo trusted Christ as his Saviour. The water of the Word had finally penetrated his dry soul, and his life has never been the same.

RECEIVING AND ASSIMILATING

Even small amounts of water penetrating desert soil can bring waiting seeds to life. But unless the water continues, the plants will quickly wither and die.

Even so, new Christians must continue to saturate their lives with the Word to grow in the Lord and bear fruit. And, to a large extent, the rate of their growth is determined by their ability to assimilate the water they receive.

We all learned the process by which plants absorb water and sunlight in elementary school. It's called *photosynthesis*. In a nutshell, it works like this: Plants take water in through their roots and carbon dioxide in through their pores, getting their energy from sunlight. In the process of assimilating the two, they release oxygen through their pores.

Photosynthesis, however, is a challenge for desert plants, because as they open their pores to release the oxygen, they also lose water through evaporation. For this reason, many desert plants only open their pores at night, and some plants actually have fewer pores, limiting both their ability to receive carbon dioxide and their risk in losing too much water. Their selective reception protects them from dehydration.

This may be fine for desert plants where water is scarce. But for the supernatural blossoms that God desires to produce in desert places, the plants must be fully open to receiving the abundant water miraculously supplied.

Christians who are selective hearers of God's Word will be stunted and dwarfed in their spiritual fruitfulness. But those whose hearts are fully open will bear fragrant blossoms and God-honoring fruit.

EARLY GROWTH

The very Sunday morning that Leo was saved, he asked to be baptized—immediately. Evelyn joined the church at the same time.

Even though the drive from Sunland to Lancaster was 125 miles round trip, the couple continued to attend faithfully. Like a thirsty sponge, Leo absorbed all the preaching and teaching he could.

The only part of Scripture that we believe is the part we obey.

Where Leo found his life to be in contradiction of the truths he heard at church, he changed. Where he realized he was lacking in obedience, he yielded. As Leo's life changed, his marriage transformed to the point he now says, "We're happier now than we've ever been."

God's Word is transformational! When you believe it and receive it, your life changes. But there's one caveat: you must submit to all of it. No selection allowed.

WHO IS IN CHARGE?

Like all successful desert gardens, the millennial desert of cascading roses and blossoming flowers is a reflection of the skilled Gardener—Christ Himself. Revelation 19:16 describes Christ as He returns to set up the Millennial Kingdom: "And he hath on his vesture and on his thigh a name written, KING OF KINGS, AND LORD OF LORDS."

Even the desert will be subject to Christ's rule.

If we want desert blossoms today, we must personally submit to His authority, acknowledging Him as the Ruler in every area of our lives.

I've seen many Christians who *say* they believe in the transforming power of God's Word, while living barren lives that in action deny Christ's authority. Truly, the only part of Scripture that we believe is the part we obey. When we *obey* His Word, our lives bring forth the sweet fragrance that only He can produce.

DESERT MUSIC

There's one other unique attribute of the millennial garden that is uncharacteristic of the natural desert—the music.

Typical desert noises, especially in the evening, can be almost haunting and mysterious: the low hoots of owls readying themselves for the night hunt, eerie howls of coyotes rallying under the moon, raspy chirps of crickets carried across the evening wind.

But when Christ reigns on Earth and transforms the desert, there will be new sounds of joyous music: "And the ransomed of the LORD shall return, and come to Zion with songs and everlasting joy upon their heads: they shall obtain joy and gladness, and sorrow and sighing shall flee away" (Isaiah 35:10).

The jubilant melodies of these songs spring from hearts that have received God's Word and freely submitted to His rule. They cannot help but rejoice. Their song is the spontaneous overflow of Christ's work in desert places.

LIVING IN THE TRANSFORMED DESERT

Leo and Evelyn continued to commute to church from Sunland for four and a half years. In that time, they put over 140,000 miles on their new car. Eventually, the couple realized they couldn't make the drive any longer and actively serve in the church. They had to choose between Sunland and Lancaster.

For many people, the choice would have been predictable and simple. Leo and Evelyn had a beautiful home in Sunland. They had lived there over fifty years. It was where they had attended junior high and high school. They had both worked and retired right there. Their family lived nearby, and they knew everyone in the community. Additionally, their gorgeous neighborhood was nestled in the foothills of the Verdugo Mountains. Why move from this security and beauty to a *desert*?

But Leo and Evelyn didn't see the choice that way. Leo looked instead at the spiritually barren years he had spent in Sunland and compared them with the fruitfulness and blessing he now knew. The couple purchased a home in Lancaster and moved in.

I don't think Leo has been bored for a day since they moved to Lancaster. Before he was saved, he was almost desperate for ways to fill his time. Now he practically lives at church. He is a church usher and our campus host for the college. He comes to the college dining hall every weekday morning at 6:30 to have breakfast with our students and invest in their lives. Additionally, he volunteers many hours each week in our media ministry, duplicating CDs and DVDs.

Leo and Evelyn have been married almost fifty-two years, and their lives, marriage, and service diffuse the sweet fragrance of Holy Spirit nurtured blossoms—a testimony to the roses God can cultivate in desert places.

DESERT ROSES

Desert blossoms aren't the result of conditions naturally disposed to growth. They are the products of God's grace, freely bestowed in unlikely places. Leo wasn't a God-fearing man who anyone would have anticipated getting saved at the age of fifty-seven. He had already rejected opportunities to respond to the Gospel and spent over thirty years in the liquor business—a picture of the classic desert heart. Yet God can plant roses even in the desert, and as Leo received the water of God's Word and trusted Christ, his life was transformed.

What God has done in literally thousands of lives here in the Mojave Desert can only be explained by one word: *grace.* Every story in this book is a powerful evidence of God's ability to grow desert gardens.

Do you minister in a desert? Do you long to see lives transformed to the glory of God? Do you desire for your own life to release a continual fragrance of grace?

Establish your heart and center your ministry on the water of God's Word. Abandon your soul to the wise authority of Christ. And, through God's grace, you will have rejoicing in desert places.

CONCLUSION

IN THIS PLACE

Not all deserts are equal. For instance, consider the variance from the Mojave here in the Southwest to the Gobi in Mongolia. Temperature, landscape, wildlife, population—they're both deserts, but they're both different.

Likewise, we've visited many different types of desert places in this book—places of ministry, need, fruitfulness, adversity, discouragement, decision. These places, like the desert itself, are each unique and varied.

But each of the desert places in this book has three common characteristics. Each was traveled by ordinary people. Each was an unlikely place. And, most importantly, each was transformed by the presence of God.

Maybe you've not experienced all of the desert places in this book. Maybe the desert place you are in today doesn't quite match the descriptions in these pages. Yet, if you are an ordinary person in an unlikely place, you too can see the transformation God's presence brings—in *any* desert place.

The message of this book is a declaration of hope for desert travelers. We serve a God who works mightily in desert places. He does not need special people or fertile opportunities. His presence alone transforms the desert. Looking back to the record of God's faithfulness displayed in these deserts gives us the courage to look around today and say, "If God could do it there and then, He can do it in *this* desert place—now."

The message of this book is also an explanation of principle. After all, not everyone sees the desert transformed. We all know people who exit the desert places of their lives staggering and dehydrated, with nothing good to say of its dusty misery.

What makes the difference? Why do some encounter the transforming presence of God in the desert and others leave defeated? The answer is simple. God can transform any desert place, but we must *acknowledge* His presence in the desert. As we've seen in the pages of Scripture, we need God more than ever in desert places. Read His Word. Trust His promises. Submit to His will. Commit to His ways. God will transform whatever desert place you find yourself in today into a place of beauty if you will let Him.

Remember the three common denominators of desert places? They are traveled by ordinary people. They are unlikely places. And they are transformed by the presence of God. Of those three elements, the only one that really makes the difference is the presence of God.

In *your* desert place, God can do the extraordinary.

Visit us online

strivingtogether.com

wcbc.edu